Praise for *Business Leader*

"This book by Frank Gallo is a reflection on his extensive experience of the country, having worked there as a senior consultant. It is sound, readable advice relevant to anyone interested in that part of the world. Gallo explores four key areas, including how to respond to the complex challenges of leading a firm or a division in China; what the major differences are in activities such as team working and decision making; and where misunderstandings can arise."

Professor Bruce Lloyd, FCMI
London South Bank University

"It seems that every day a new book on doing business in China is written. Now, a new book has arrived on the scene that is a 'must read.' *Business Leadership in China* by Frank T. Gallo is like a textbook on how to blend best Western practices with Chinese wisdom. This timely book will ensure a harmonious leadership style that draws out the best from both Western and Chinese business practices."

Russ M. Miller, LLIF
Chairman and CEO, Performance Institute

"Frank Gallo recently published an outstanding book, *Business Leadership in China*. The book sheds light on the uniqueness of China's business leadership, the clash of old and new generation leaders, and its transition to hybrid management leadership practices. By sharing his own experiences of consulting in China, he provides practical advice and examples of how Chinese business leaders think and act."

Editor
Korea Times

"Dr. Gallo's book is a 'Little Red Book' based on his experience and observation. Not only does it analyze the influence of culture and tradition on leadership style, but also helps Chinese leaders more deeply understand the Western leadership concept and practices. Every foreign leader and every domestic leader should read this book and benefit from it. I highly recommend this insightful and empowering book."

Gary Wang
Founder and CEO, MindSpan Learning

"Dr. Frank Gallo's book illustrates the differences and similarities of culture, leadership, and management style between Chinese and foreign executives. It is of great value to multinationals who are planning to enter the China market and Chinese companies who are about to go abroad."

Gao Yong
Founder and President, Career International Inc.

"Dr. Gallo observes the influence of leaders and leadership in Chinese companies. Written from the perspective of an American scholar and leadership expert, this book will help foreigners understand Chinese companies and the business climate as well as provide insightful views for Chinese leaders."

Guo Xin
Asia Chief Executive, Mercer HR Capital Consultancy

"Dr. Gallo's book is a classic work that really 'digs into the earth.' As a Chinese and a 25-year business leader, I am deeply touched by his insightful and interesting observations about the behaviors of Chinese leaders. This book allowed me to see a different view of Chinese leadership that comes from a Westerner's cultural perspective. The book provides important guidance for understanding the art of leadership for companies operating in the China market, both multinational and domestic."

Patrick Huang
Greater China President, Towers Watson Consulting

"China does not lack leadership ideology and philosophy, but lacks the tools to implement strategy. In contrast, the West has abundant leadership theories and practices, but lacks an understanding of and insight into Chinese culture. No matter whether you are in China or other countries, if you want to be an effective leader, you need to have the right local knowledge and apply that to best practices. The author analyzes Chinese culture and its business environment with a modest and open mind. In his many years of leading, teaching, and consulting, he demonstrates how to combine the philosophies of the East with the business practices of the West. I believe this book will inspire Chinese and Western leaders alike."

Chris Xu
Director of Human Resources and Leadership
Development, TCL Corporation

BUSINESS LEADERSHIP IN CHINA

HOW TO BLEND BEST WESTERN PRACTICES WITH CHINESE WISDOM

(REVISED EDITION)

BUSINESS LEADERSHIP IN CHINA

HOW TO BLEND BEST WESTERN PRACTICES WITH CHINESE WISDOM

(REVISED EDITION)

FRANK T. GALLO

WILEY

John Wiley & Sons (Asia) Pte. Ltd.

Other Wiley Editorial Offices

John Wiley & Sons, 111 River Street, Hoboken, NJ 07030, USA

John Wiley & Sons, The Atrium, Southern Gate, Chichester, West Sussex, P019 8SQ, United Kingdom

John Wiley & Sons (Canada) Ltd., 5353 Dundas Street West, Suite 400, Toronto, Ontario, M9B 6HB, Canada

John Wiley & Sons Australia Ltd, 42 McDougall Street, Milton, Queensland 4064, Australia

Wiley-VCH, Boschstrasse 12, D-69469 Weinheim, Germany

Library of Congress Cataloging-in-Publication Data

ISBN 978-0-47082730-7

Typeset in 11/13.5pt Fairfield LT Std Light by MPS Limited, a Macmillan Company
Printed in Singapore by Saik Wah Press Pte Ltd

10 9 8 7 6 5 4 3 2 1

CONTENTS

ACKNOWLEDGMENTS

The terrific business leaders and China leadership experts who allowed me to interview them contributed greatly to this book. They are described in detail in Appendix 1, but here is a list of their names, titles, and corporate affiliations: Bob Aubrey, Ph.D., Chairman and Founder, Metizo, Singapore; Bin Gong, Asia Pacific Regional HR Director, Bayer HealthCare, Hong Kong; Ruby Chen, Director of the McKinsey Leadership Institute in China, McKinsey & Company, Beijing; Ding Jingping, Ph.D., Senior Partner and Vice President, Pan Pacific Management Institute, Beijing; Kevin Fong, Chief Executive Officer, China Automobile Association, Beijing; (Wallacy) Gao Yong, President, Career International, Beijing; Guo Xin, Greater China Managing Director, Mercer Human Resource Consulting, Beijing; Hala Helmy, President, Mundipharma, Beijing; Patrick Huang, Greater China Managing Director, Watson Wyatt Worldwide, Shanghai; Victor Lang, President, MMD Asia Pacific, Beijing; Jim Leininger, General Manager, Watson Wyatt Worldwide, Beijing; (James) Li Jianbo, Vice President, Human Resources, Cisco Systems (China), Beijing; Ren Binyan, Ph.D., Vice President, Alcoa (China) Investment Company, Ltd., Beijing; Charles Shao, Beijing Director of Leadership, Hewitt Associates, Beijing; Shi Lan, Senior Consultant, Towers Perrin, Beijing; Kelly Wang, Founder and Director, GW Technologies Co., Ltd., Beijing; Angie Wei, Senior Leadership Consultant, Hewitt Associates, Beijing; (Chris) Xu Fang, Vice President, TCL Institute of Leadership Development, TCl Corporation, Huizhou; Yi Min,

Director of Global Leadership and Organization Development, Lenovo Group, Raleigh, North Carolina; and Janet Zhong, Vice President, Human Resources, Alcoa (China) Investment Company, Ltd., Beijing. There is no way this book could have been written without them. My thanks to each of them.

Bob Aubrey, in addition to being interviewed for the book, also provided invaluable information on the Western viewpoint on Chinese leadership, as well as advice on how to present the material. Dr. Aubrey also served as a senior advisor to me on this project.

Of the many others who have contributed to the writing of this book, I want to give special thanks to (Sally) Xue Gong for her assistance in translating, interpreting, and abstracting the Chinese literature on leadership. I would also like to extend my gratitude to Adeline Lim, Janis Soo, Fiona Wong, and their colleagues at John Wiley & Sons (Asia) for keeping me on time and on target. Special thanks to Robyn Flemming for applying her fantastic copyediting skills in this revised edition.

Michelle Wang of Metizo and Li Yong of Mercer Human Resource Consulting provided technical advice on, and explanations of, many of the Chinese terms used in the text. (Richard) Xu Yue also provided technical advice, as well as help in securing several interviews with Chinese leaders.

Wang Ling of Calypso provided invaluable administrative assistance throughout this endeavor; and her son, Wang Gao, gave me enormous inspiration.

Finally, I would like to thank Mutsuko and Brian Gallo for their unfailing support, encouragement, and love.

Author's note: Names are presented as they are most often used by the person mentioned. Chinese names are listed with the family name first and the given name second. Western names are listed with the given name first and the family name second. Names of Chinese people with Western given names are presented in the Western style: given name first, followed by the family name.

PREFACE TO THE REVISED EDITION

As this book is about to go to press, we are hearing some very disturbing news from southern China. Taiwan-owned Foxconn, one of the world's largest makers of mobile phones, has already experienced 10 employee suicides this year. And we are only halfway through the year. There have been several theories put forward in an attempt to explain what could be causing this terrible phenomenon. They include the very long working hours, having to live away from home, and the high stress levels brought on by tight deadlines. The chairman of Foxconn seems to have his heart in the right place and has made changes aimed at improving the situation. The company has hired about 100 mental health counselors and installed safety nets at its dormitories and factories. It also is reportedly planning to increase salary levels dramatically. But in my view, these interventions will only alleviate the symptoms, not the causes, of the suicides.

Foxconn is not the only company in the world to experience this kind of tragedy. But the high number of suicides occurring over a very short period, in a company with very stressful working conditions, must make one wonder if the tragic outcome could have been avoided if supervisors were just as concerned about their employees' well-being as they are about production quotas. How well trained are the company's team leaders to help moderate workplace stress among their team members? My guess is that supervisors and team leaders in many companies in China are being forced to focus on production, and not on the needs of their employees. Pressure from clients is passed on to senior management, from where it flows downstream. By the time it gets to the front-line employee, there is no further place for it to go.

In my experience in China, first-line supervisors and team leaders are very young and inexperienced in managing others. In fact, many of them have never had role models, or coaching or mentoring in how to manage others. They are selected primarily for their technical abilities. When a people-oriented issue arises, their first reaction is to report the problem to a very overworked human resources department. It is not that they don't care about their employees; it is more a case of they don't know what else to do.

Every fast-growing company in China with a large sales force or manufacturing force to manage is experiencing this problem of manager competency. Until the problem is fixed, those companies are at great risk for the sort of serious consequences that Foxconn is currently experiencing.

We cannot instantaneously make this problem go away. China is growing like nowhere else in the world. Well-meaning young people are being forced to take on people management responsibilities that, in other countries, are usually given to people 10 years senior to them. The only way I can see to fix the problem is through better preparation of these very young supervisors. I hope that some of the concepts examined in this book will be a useful beginning for many of those aspiring leaders.

* * *

It has been three years since I wrote the first edition of *Business Leadership in China*. During that time, I have had the privilege of receiving comments from many readers that of who have helped me to refine my own thinking and observations on leadership in China. Some readers helped me to better understand Chinese history and the wisdom that it can continue to offer. Others were eager to share their own stories about experiences similar to those mentioned in the book. When appropriate, I have tried to modify the book based on those insightful comments.

Perhaps the most valuable learning for me came from many of the book's Chinese readers, especially in relation to the unique traits of Chinese leaders described in Chapter Six. Many readers commented that traits such as *wu* (悟) and *zhong yong* (中庸) were so ingrained in their daily thinking, they barely realized they were using them. When I saw that some Chinese leaders were thinking anew about how they use their unique Chinese traits, I felt a sense of accomplishment from the first edition that I did not expect.

A moment of truth that I had experienced in 2005 led me to write the book in the first place. I was teaching an M.B.A. course in Beijing entitled "Motivating Employees in China." The course, which was being taught at a well-known university, was designed to teach Chinese managers and future leaders in China how to apply Western best-practice leadership techniques to their daily management in China. For several weeks, the students listened politely. There were often questions, but they were always about content, never about its applicability in the Chinese context.

Then, one night, someone told me something surprising. He said that he understood and appreciated all that I was teaching him, but he feared that none of it would work in his firm. He was a manager in a state-owned enterprise, he said, where employees were conditioned to believe that he was interested only in their performance—not in their welfare. Others in the class, emboldened by this brave student's remarks, agreed with his position. The classroom discussion thereafter became much more lively than usual, as we all tried to figure out how to apply these obviously Western ideas and practices to Chinese businesses. I had underestimated how difficult the process might be, and the students had initially assumed it would not be possible to apply them in the Chinese context. The idea that it might be feasible to do so was clearly new to them. No one doubted the success of these approaches in Western firms. They just felt that it would now be their job to try and figure out how to use these ideas in China.

Ever since then, I have devoted my learning to understanding how to do this. This book is a compilation of those thoughts and, I hope, a first step in the direction of integrating the best leadership practices of the West with the complexity, contrasts, and ancient wisdom of China.

While the business processes in most multinational firms operating in China are more like those found in the West, the firms themselves are still strongly influenced by their Chinese employees. Some of these employees are young and not dominated by older Chinese thinking, but most are old enough to at least have been influenced by it. As such, the Western-educated leader coming into a firm in China, even one that is multinational, is bound to meet with some subtle resistance.

This book is written primarily for the person who already has some familiarity with China and its complex culture. Many of the concepts and the various traits described in Chapter Six are best understood if the reader has already lived in China and can relate to how different the daily pace is from that in Western countries. However, it should also serve as a primer for any non-Chinese person who is interested in working in a management role in China. If the reader simply tried to understand the various key concepts of Chinese leadership that are mentioned throughout the text and summarized in Appendix 2, he or she would be further ahead than I was when I arrived in China in 2001. I had 30 years of business and management experience, so I thought I had sufficient grounding in how to manage. What I failed to realize was what a different type of place China is from anywhere I had lived before.

The book will also be of value to Chinese business people and students of business or human resources in China who wish to get a first-hand look at how Westerners view leadership in China and how they practice their craft.

The book is not designed to compete with the many sociological and anthropological studies that have preceded it. For very comprehensive global research on cultural differences in business, the reader is referred to Geert Hofstede's seminal work, *Culture and Organizations: Software of the Mind*,[1] and his earlier work with Michael Bond that is focused on China and refers specifically to the influence of Confucianism on business, *Confucius and Economic Growth: New Trends in Culture's Consequences*.[2]

Perhaps the most comprehensive view of global cultural differences among leaders is the GLOBE (Global Leadership and Organizational Effectiveness) study. It is presented in *Culture,*

Leadership and Organizations, whose lead author is Robert J. House.[3] In this study, House and his colleagues describe many of the specific differences between leaders in various cultures. One of the key factors of relevance to this work is their research on power-distance, the relative distance between a leader and his or her followers. This one issue has enormous impact when comparing Chinese and Western leadership practices and will be discussed in detail in the book.

This book relied on those sources, as well as many others from the Western and Chinese business literature (see Bibliography). But more importantly, I have had the benefit of interviews with 20 Chinese business leaders who gave me practical insights into how they lead in China. Finally, for better or worse, I have added my own voice, based on my experiences in China as a corporate leader, a teacher, an executive coach, and a consultant.

Frank T. Gallo, Ph.D.
September, 2010

Notes

1 Geert Hofstede, *Culture and Organizations: Software of the Mind* (London: McGraw-Hill, 1991).
2 Geert Hofstede and Michael Bond, "Confucius and Economic Growth: New Trends in Culture's Consequences," *Organizational Dynamics*, Vol. 16, No. 4, 1988, pp. 4–21.
3 Robert J. House, *et al.*, *Culture, Leadership and Organizations* (Thousand Oaks, CA: Sage Publications, 2004).

FOREWORD

It is with great pleasure that I contribute a foreword to Frank Gallo's exciting new book on business leadership in China. While there are many books written by Westerners about leadership, and many others written by Chinese authors, none of them applies the formula that Gallo has used to mix the best of the West with the best of Chinese thinking.

The book has value for at least three business groups. The first, of course, are the many foreign leaders who come to China and try to make things work here. As Gallo points out, many of them fail. They do so because they believe that they can simply take what they have learned about leadership in their home country and apply it here in China. That formula will not work. Gallo introduces the example of empowerment, a very common Western leadership best practice. While empowerment can be quite successfully implemented in China, it usually requires first an explanation as to why it is such a valued practice in the West, and why it is also potentially important for business in China. Numerous studies have shown how empowerment enriches jobs and leads to better productivity; this information is all that should be necessary to get most Chinese employees to buy in. But when an unfamiliar Western concept is introduced without any reason being given, some employees may become suspicious. There are several examples in the book of how Western leaders empowered employees without giving them adequate explanation first. In most cases, the attempts led to ridicule of the leader.

Is he too weak to understand how to do this himself?

Is she a lazy leader who just wants me to do her job?

Is there some hidden meaning to this change in my job? Maybe my boss wants to see me fail?

After all, Confucianists in China have taught that *jun jun chen chen fu fu zi zi* (君君臣臣 父父子子, when the king is king, the minister is minister, the father is father, and the son is son, then there will be order in the society.) Anything that potentially distorts the chosen role of the leader may be a mistake.

The second business group for whom the book provides value is Chinese managers and leaders. While many of the Chinese concepts discussed in the text, as well as some of the Western leadership concepts, are known to current Chinese leaders, the challenge remains of how to integrate these into a formula that works here in China, especially when we work with foreigners— either as colleagues in a multinational firm or a joint venture, or as customers for our Chinese-made products and services. The understanding the book provides of how the two cultures can integrate best practices from all over the world makes it a "must read" for Chinese leaders in China.

The third business group is the human resources community, either in China or in the West. If the company needs to blend leaders from Chinese and Western cultures, then it must also integrate an understanding of the cultural foundations that make them different, as well as those that make them similar. Oftentimes when there is a cultural struggle in a company, the task is placed on the human resources department to make it work better. This book has enormous value in helping with that task.

I am a native and life-long resident of China. For over 20 years I have been working with Western firms and Western employees. In my current work as the Managing Director of Hewitt's Greater China practice, I also oversee the leadership consulting practice. In my experience, the needs of both Chinese and Western leaders in China are quite similar. In fact, Hewitt's research on leadership indicates four common elements that describe a great company for leaders. The first is that the leaders lead the way. There is an unwavering commitment from the senior team to build and manage future leaders. The second is an unrelenting focus on talent. Companies need to assess, develop, train, and pay differently for their top talent as compared to average employees. Third is a company's ability to align its leadership programs with its business strategy. Companies that lose sight of that alignment become confused and often lose the way. Companies that follow this approach have a leadership strategy that is well aligned with their business strategy, and this makes leading a clear approach in the firm for both the leaders and those who must follow. Finally, the element that truly brings a firm over the top of other firms is that leadership has become an organizational discipline. The way one leads is engrained in everything the leader does.

These four elements (sometimes referred to as "leadership truths") have been constant for the many years Hewitt has conducted its "Top Companies for Leaders" surveys. Furthermore, these truths have been shown to be relevant in all geographic markets—and certainly including China. However, when it comes down to the behaviors that individual leaders in China must follow, they need to learn to modify what they do in order to be most effective here. Even a company that religiously follows the four truths must ensure that their leaders do not use old patterns learned in other places or at other times. *Business Leadership in China* describes how to shed those old patterns and lead in the way that is required in China today. This is why I strongly believe that *Business Leadership in China* is a "must read" for all leaders in China and everyone who aspires to be one.

Jenny Li
Hewitt Associates,
Managing Director for Greater China
Beijing, China
2010

A PERSONAL STORY

I came to China for the first time in the summer of 2001. I had been working in Boston at Watson Wyatt[1], one of the top human resource consulting firms in the world. I was only a few years away from retirement, but I was asked by my company to take on the role of managing director for China. Although I had never lived in China before, I was extremely excited about what I considered to be a once-in-a-lifetime opportunity. It would be like going back to the time of the US Industrial Revolution, I thought; only, I would have the benefit of all that I knew and be able to use that knowledge to improve our business in China. Also, I have had an affinity for Asia since the late 1960s, when I lived in Japan and came to appreciate firsthand the importance of culture in life and the way we make our decisions. In a word, I was thrilled.

While Watson Wyatt had maintained a presence on the China mainland since the 1970s, for most of that time, it was controlled from Hong Kong. Our understanding of China then was strongly influenced by Hong Kong impressions based on old history and, often, bad memories. Employees went to the mainland as the need arose, but we did not have our first full-time presence there until the mid-1990s when we opened an office in Shanghai. This was soon followed by another office in Beijing. Both of these offices were very successful in generating business. Actually, the phone never stopped ringing. By 2001, it was time to get serious and turn these two independent Chinese offices into the Chinese arm of this global professional service firm. There was plenty to do in terms of coordination and integration. But the task was very doable.

When I was selected to run the operation, our strategy was to increase market share and become the market leader among Chinese local companies. My company, and certainly I, believed then (and I still do now) that China would be the future center for world business. It was not so farfetched to imagine that within 20 years, our company would be heavily weighted with China revenue. We needed to make a stake in China while the field was still so green. Our foremost goal was to establish ourselves in China as the market leader and try to hold on to that lead for as long as possible. My job was to coordinate activities here and help get the wheel turning in an organized way so that we could reach our market share targets while teaching our Chinese employees and clients about our corporate values and technical know-how. In those days, we were willing to sacrifice profit to get the business. The strong desire to be profitable came later, but in the first few years of the century, our clear goal was to gain market share.

The consultants on the ground here were the ones who brought in most of the business, especially among local Chinese companies. My primary responsibility with those clients was to meet and greet top leaders in the client firm, establish a sense of confidence that we were best suited to do the job, and give them my solemn commitment to meet their needs in this very challenging and dynamic market.

But soon after I arrived, I noticed a significant problem during the price negotiation stage. I tried very hard to give clients what I truly believed was a fair price in return for excellent work. The work was always aimed at making the client companies more effective in the area of human resources, and therefore more competitive in the market—for both product and talent. But no matter what I tried, I always left the negotiations feeling like I had lost. Since our corporate strategy for China was to gain the highest market share, we were sometimes willing to give fairly steep discounts. But even when we did this, clients still wanted more. Sometimes the request was so outrageous that we walked away from the deal. But most of the time, we continued to compromise in order to win the business. We were successful and did continue to grow, but it soon became apparent that profits were not right around the corner as we had all originally thought. The pull from clients for more and more service within the original contract terms became a very worrisome challenge for me.

After about six months of haggling with clients and spending long nights at the office commiserating with our managers and finance staff, I had a kind of epiphany. It came while I was having a drink one evening with one of my very bright Chinese employees. She said, "Frank, you are never going to beat these people. You are too nice and too honest. What you need to recognize is that the managers you are bargaining with are trying to squeeze you for all you are worth. While you are looking for a win–win, they are looking to win at your expense. You have to either play the same game or accept that you will not reach your goals in China."

This conversation had a lasting impact on my work in China. It is not something that Westerners usually come here knowing. Rather, we trust the negotiating strategy that we developed in our home countries—a strategy based on a "win–win" philosophy. It occurred to me (finally!) that my clients and I were playing by totally different sets of rules. The Chinese managers I was negotiating with were playing a game of "win–lose."

The "win–win" approach is based on a concept of trust that is less commonly found in China than in the West. In China, trust is extremely strong within the family and among close friends—perhaps even stronger than in the West. But as one moves further from the inner circle of family and friends, the amount of trust tends to diminish. While this is found in most cultures, it is particularly evident in China. Chinese executives often expect the person they are negotiating with to be "untrustworthy." They are usually unwilling to believe that someone would actually consider offering a "fair" price for something unless they have worked together previously and have established some form of *guan xi* (关系, very close relationship) that, in turn, would lead to more trust.

Like many others before me in China, I was forced to change my own rules of engagement. I would discuss price negotiations first with my Chinese managers. We would then develop a scenario for how to conduct the negotiations. We had our entry price, our margin for bargaining, and our bottom price. In order to achieve some profit, the entry price needed to be extremely unrealistic.

But we learned that until we had enough of a trusting relationship with the client, we could not expect to receive a fair price for our work based solely on honest costing spreadsheets.

I am very happy to say that, after working in China for more than nine years and developing trusting relationships, I no longer need to play this game. I state a price for my work and declare very clearly what I will do for that price. While some clients may still attempt some minor bargaining, I usually counter these with offers to reduce the scope of the work supplied, rather than drop the price. However, a new leader in China, without his or her own strong relationships that have been developed over time, will have a very difficult time getting to this point. To make money in China, you must be able to show that you are serious about being here; that you will do an honest day's work, and the customer will get what they need for the price agreed upon. No one can achieve that here with smooth talk or corporate reputation alone. This country, more than anywhere else I have worked, insists that you put your money where your mouth is. No more, no less.

I share this story to make the point that even someone with the best intentions, someone with higher-than-average emotional intelligence, could still fall into the cultural trap that ensnares many Western managers. It is not a matter of ethnocentrism. Rather, it is about getting deeper and deeper into a country's psyche in order to understand why one's own long-held and trusted beliefs about best practices may be put to the test. It is not that they are wrong; they are just for another time and place.

Note

1   In 2010, Watson Wyatt merged with Towers Perrin and is now known as Towers Watson.

UNDERSTANDING LEADERSHIP IN CHINA TODAY

*"Some Westerners don't seem to fully understand
the Asian leadership virtue of being tender in
appearance and resolute in mind."*
UN Secretary General Ban Ki Moon
(*in response to the Western press referring
to him as a "low-key" leader*)

Introduction to Part I

The first part of this book provides some background on business leadership in China, based on my experiences as a leader and as an observer of business in China. It also offers a guide on how to use the book, whether the reader is an existing leader in China or a student in the classroom.

Chapter One lays the foundation for the book and describes the three key themes. It also explains what is meant by "Chinese wisdom," which is fundamental to the book's themes and is part of the book's subtitle. It also provides examples from my own experience of some of the cultural differences that exist between Western and Chinese firms.

Chapter Two examines the book's methodology and explains how to use it. Chapter Three takes a look at the leadership needs that are especially relevant in China. Chapters Four through Seven provide important background information on why leaders in China behave as they do. Chapters Four and Five explain in some detail the different cultural foundations that make up a Westerner's view on leadership versus those of a Chinese leader. Chapter Six describes and examines a list of unique traits that existing Chinese leaders have identified as being important in China and which differ from those found in the West.

Chapter Seven is a new chapter for this revised edition of the book. It is entitled "Leading from the Heart," and identifies a unique trait of some of China's most admired leaders. It also describes leadership styles found in many other Chinese leaders.

The final chapter in Part I reviews the most common human resource trends in China, and examines how these impact on leadership in China, as discussed in Part II.

Some readers may decide to skip some of the chapters in Part II that are not relevant to their particular company or assignment. But it is recommended that Part I be read in its entirety, as it lays the foundation for the rest of the book.

Chapter 1

INTRODUCTION

The quotation that opens this chapter, which appeared in a popular Beijing newspaper, is very telling about life in China today. Years ago, one would not admit to having made a mistake, as there could be serious consequences. Today, as Chinese thinking merges more and more with that of the West, it is becoming more common to admit to one's mistakes. But the long-held fear of being wrong continues, as the second part of the quotation indicates. It is okay to be wrong about something once, but not twice. In China, one works very hard to be right. Sometimes, to avoid being wrong, a Chinese person will choose not to act.

This topic takes us to the subject of business leadership. What does it take to be a great leader in China? What is different about leadership in China compared to elsewhere in the world? Leadership is a huge issue for businesses in China, especially today. This book is intended to provide answers to those questions, as well as to outline what companies in China—both foreign and local firms—can do now to improve the abilities of their leaders.

Thousands of books have been written on business leadership. Many of these have been translated into Chinese and have been read by Chinese business people. China has an enormous need to improve the quality of its leadership, and its current and future leaders have a craving for information that will help them get to the top. But my Chinese friends tell me that, while they find these

Western works intellectually stimulating, there always seems to be something missing. Western concepts and leadership practices differ in their relevance to and workability in the Chinese context. It would be naïve for anyone to think otherwise. But that is just what many of these Western books do.

In the final chapter, we take a look at one of the best-known Western books on leadership, *Leadership Challenge* by James Kouzes and Barry Posner.[1] We examine the five features of their well-known leadership model and identify which aspects of the model work well in China, which need some modification, and which should simply be discarded for China.

This book makes several assumptions that can be condensed into three major themes: (1) Chinese business leadership is in need of improvement. (2) Simply importing best Western practices for leadership will not work in China. (3) Leaders in China need to blend best Western practices with Chinese wisdom.

Theme #1: Chinese Business Leadership is in Need of Improvement

There are countless stories and much has been written on the need to improve the standard of business leadership in China. While there are several possible reasons for this, the main ones are the relatively recent change to a market economy from the previous Soviet-style planned economy, and the consequent inexperience of China's business managers and leaders in terms of how to operate in such an economy. In a planned economy business, there is very little for the leader to do other than to ensure that the wishes of his or her superiors are carried out. That means meeting production quotas (if they exist) and ensuring that there are ample jobs for those people being lobbied for by the central or provincial government. There is very little need to motivate employees to be better-performing workers, as is the case in a market economy. Likewise, the focus of planned economy leaders tends to be upward (toward the Party and the government), rather than downward toward the workforce.

Theme #2: Simply Importing Best Western Leadership Practices Will Not Work in China

Many Western leadership experts have visited China to give lectures and sell their books. But the problem is that these books were nearly all written with a Western mindset for Western leaders managing businesses in Western countries. As will be discussed in great detail throughout this book, most of these practices, while possibly very effective in the West, need to be modified extensively if they are to work in China. In fact, many of them will never work well here. There are cultural differences between China and the West in the way workers view their leaders, what they expect from their leaders, and what leaders can expect from their workforce. Furthermore, there are very fundamental differences in how life works in China compared to the West. Some of the values that Westerners hold dear are frowned upon in China. Western leaders who uphold those values in China will often fail in China. Their intentions may be good, but the way they are perceived in China can spell disaster for a business.

Theme #3: Leaders in China Need to Blend Best Western Practices with Chinese Wisdom

The best leaders in China, be they Westerners or Chinese, have learned how to blend the best of Western leadership practices with traditional Chinese wisdom. There are countless examples of this in this book as we describe the practices of current executives who are doing well here. One common example that I will expound on at some length later is the different way empowerment is used in China compared to in the West. In the West, most management gurus advise giving employees the opportunity to truly "own" their jobs by empowering them with the ability to make decisions, take action, and generate results, without needing to gain approval from a superior. But in China, where relationships operate according to a Confucian hierarchy, this approach may not have the anticipated effect. Recently arrived Western executives who, with the best of intentions, want to make their employees feel enriched in their work by empowering them with new authority and responsibility, are often surprised by the negative (or at best, neutral) reactions their efforts receive. Many Chinese employees, especially those who are new to Western management ideas, are often quite confused by the role distortion brought on by empowerment. "Why is the boss asking me to do something that he or she is better at? Is he or she trying to make me fail? Is he or she not really that good at this and therefore wanting to place future blame on me?" Chinese workers are generally quite polite and would not confront their new boss about this directly. So, often, the employee simply does not act at all. When the boss, who expected certain results, finds that nothing has been accomplished, he or she feels disappointed and frustrated and begins to question the performance value of the Chinese workforce.

Throughout this book, these three themes will recur. They will be evident in excerpts from the literature, and in anecdotes shared by the executives who were interviewed, and will be discussed in detail as I describe my own experiences as a Westerner leading in China.

What is Chinese Wisdom?

The wisdom that is often relied upon (perhaps subconsciously) by many Chinese leaders comes from several sources. Most notably, it is founded in Confucianism and its many offshoots, such as Neo-Confucianism, which mixes traditional Confucianism with Buddhism, and New Confucianism, which began in the twentieth century and tries to link traditional Confucian thought with the future. It is also deeply embedded in the Daoist and Buddhist literature. Chinese Buddhism can be broken down into the primary form of Buddhism practiced in China, known as Han Buddhism, Tibetan Buddhism (also known as Lamaism), and Southern Buddhism, which is practiced by the Dai people in Yunnan province.

But Chinese wisdom also comes from other non-religious sources. *The Art of War*, by Sun Zi[2] (known commonly in the West as Sun Tzu), is often quoted in both English- and Chinese-language works on leadership, as are the writings and sayings of Chinese leaders such as Sun Yat Sen, Deng Xiaoping, and Mao Zedong. Finally, especially among older leaders in China and those who manage state-owned enterprises (SOEs), we sometimes see the influence of the former Soviet Union's planned-economy approach.

Many of the leadership theories that are imposed on the Chinese from the West are, as Geert Hofstede comments, "based on the assumption that leadership consists basically of dyadic relationships between leaders and followers. This is clearly a reflection of the individualistic orientation of dominant mainstream US culture."[3] Does this make sense in China? Hofstede says that China is a high power-distance culture, while the US is a low power-distance culture.[4] The House study confirms this view.[5] In simple terms, this means that in low power-distance cultures such as the US and many Western European countries, you can expect a close relationship between a leader and a follower. In a high power-distance culture such as China, the opposite is true: There is often no expectation of any personal relationship between the leader and the follower. If this is true of China, how can we expect Chinese leaders to care about empathizing with, empowering, and relating well to their employees? These interpersonal skills are not a necessary aspect of leading in a traditional Chinese business. Yet, all of our Western leadership books emphasize their importance in making us better leaders. The problem is that Westerners who try this in China often fall on their faces. Many Chinese leaders will not try them because they know intuitively that they will not work.

A simple way to make this point is to ask Westerners how close their relationship is with the president of their country. My guess is that more than 99 percent of them will say it is not close at all and they do not expect it ever to be close. What I expect from my country's president is that he or she does what needs to be done to keep us safe, healthy, and economically sound. I do not expect to have a warm and empathetic relationship with the president, nor do I count on him or her to personally coach me in how to become a better person. Even in a low power-distance society, we have our limits. We do not expect our top leaders to be available to us. The relationship that Westerners have with the heads of their countries is often analogous to the relationship that Chinese business employees have with their corporate leaders. They may have a close relationship with their supervisors, but they do not expect to have such a relationship with those at the top of the firm. It is just not how things are typically done in China.

Let me give you another example from my career. In the 1980s, I worked for Wang Laboratories in Massachusetts. This was a very successful high-tech company that was founded by a Chinese immigrant. Dr. An Wang was an outstanding entrepreneur who basically invented what became known as the word processor. His chief financial officer (CFO) and several other confidantes were Chinese nationals, giving the firm a strong Chinese influence. The firm did not really feel like a Western firm.

In the 1980s, personal computers with built-in word processing software were just starting to hit the market. But for at least a decade prior to that, Wang Laboratories was the leader in word processing hardware and software. As IBM began to make its mark on the personal computer industry, specialist machines like those made by Wang quickly became dinosaurs. The company started bleeding money. The company was eventually forced to replace Dr. An Wang, the legendary founder and soul of the company, with a new chief executive officer (CEO), Richard W. Miller, who came with a rich résumé and was expected to introduce a more American approach to doing business than the Chinese-run company had adopted. One of the first things he did was to eliminate the hierarchical distance between executives and the regular employees. He broke down the organizational structure and pretty much dissolved what was known in the Wang Towers as "the Penthouse" and moved functional leaders closer to their groups. He then closed the executive dining room and required the executives to eat with the rest of the employees. Finally, he eliminated the executive parking lot, which meant executives had to come to work early if they wanted a parking spot near the building. Otherwise, they would have to jockey for position with all of the security guards, kitchen workers, and administrative underlings like me. In other words, he tried to change the power-distance from high (as it was in China) to low (as it was in the US).

Miller did not last very long. Within a relatively short time, Wang Laboratories filed for bankruptcy under Chapter 11 and Miller was gone. The reasons for the company's failure were complex, but mostly had to do with the way the industry was moving into personal computers. Nonetheless, the cultural impact of Miller's autocratic style and the changes he imposed hastened the departure of many of Wang Laboratories' top talents. The changes were seen as radical and led to major turmoil in the workforce at all levels.

So, what is the lesson? Even in America, if you have a company founded on a Chinese form of power-distance, you cannot easily convert to a Western approach of low power-distance. If it is so hard to do this successfully in America, how hard must it be in China?

This process of blending best Western leadership practices with Chinese wisdom is not just like making soup, where you can blend this with that and come up with a tasty broth. Rather, it is much more like a salad, where every ingredient retains its individual taste. Some ingredients mix together nicely, and some need quite a bit of additional seasoning. Alas, some ingredients can actually spoil the salad. So it is with Western leadership practices. Some of them fit quite well in China. Some need a bit of modification before they can be included in the leader's toolbox. Like a spoiled salad, some of them just do not work in China.

This is the essence of this book: Take the key leadership concepts and practices that have been introduced from the West and decide how they can best be integrated with traditional Chinese wisdom and classical Chinese leadership. Which Western practices work well here? Which ones do not? Which ones need a little more seasoning to make them mix well?

My intention is to combine my knowledge of Western leadership approaches with that of Chinese business culture and make a leadership salad that tastes great and complements the business meal.

As explained earlier, empowerment, which is taken for granted in the West, is not so easily accomplished in a hierarchical culture like China whose citizens have been raised according to a Confucianist philosophy that preaches order and precise role definition. Flat organizations and matrix management require a conceptual leap for most people who have been raised in this way. In a later chapter, I will suggest how to make such practices work in China.

Another example is trust. How do Westerners and the Chinese view trust differently, and how do these different views impact on leadership styles? Most Westerners have been raised to have a kind of formal trust in a system where everyone in a company shares the same basic values and principles, which should be adhered to in order to move the company in a certain direction. In China, however, trust operates much more on a personal level. Personal trust needs to be earned. Until it is earned, some of the concepts that are so common in Western business thinking cannot easily be understood. This often leads to very wrong impressions about what is going on. While the Westerner might conclude that his or her Chinese counterpart is not trustworthy, the Chinese will often view the Westerner as rash and rude in thinking that they can move forward as quickly as the Westerner wishes without having first established a closer personal relationship.

Another example of the differences has to do with change. Westerners, generally, think change is good. We frequently change jobs, move house, and trade in our cars. We even have very high divorce rates. Chinese, on the other hand, are more inclined to stay put—in their firms, their homes, and their families. While there is a trend away from this, especially in jobs in China, it is still a much more traditional society than many in the West. As such, employees in China often express dissatisfaction with their firms and their leaders if change is too frequent. While employees in the West may have similar feelings about what they perceive to be too much change, it is such a common way of life that their tolerance for change-oriented leaders tends to be greater than in China.

A final example distinguishes between "doing" and just "being." Westerners climb a mountain with one purpose in mind: to get to the top. Easterners can climb a mountain every day and never reach the top but still be extremely satisfied with the experience of just being on the mountain. In the US, we try to make the point about the importance of "stopping to smell the roses." Most Westerners, especially Western leaders, hardly notice that the flowers are there. This is one area where both cultures might benefit from each other. Western leaders in China could worry less about results and more about the process. But at the same time, in this new global economy, Chinese leaders need to focus more on results.

So, these are some of the cultural differences we see between China and the West. When you apply these differences to how people in business think, you can see how they can also shape the way people lead. That is why it is so important for Westerners to modify their thinking about how to lead in China. Likewise, the challenge rests with Chinese leaders to learn how to take the best practices from Western leadership and apply them appropriately in China.

Notes

1 James M. Kouzes and Barry Y. Posner, *The Leadership Challenge*, 3rd edition (San Francisco: Jossey-Bass, 2002).
2 Sun Zi, *The Art of War* (Internet; English translation found on various public websites).
3 Romie F. Littrell, "Desirable Leadership Behaviors of Multi-Cultural Managers in China," *Journal of Management Development*, Vol. 21, No. 1, 2002, pp. 5–74 at p. 11.
4 Geert Hofstede, *Culture and Organizations: Software of the Mind*, (London: McGraw-Hill, 1991).
5 Robert J. House, *et al.*, *Culture, Leadership and Organizations* (Thousand Oaks, CA: Sage Publications, 2004).

Chapter One Executive Summary

Introduction

- This book has three pervasive themes: (1) Chinese business leadership is in need of improvement; (2) simply importing best Western practices for leadership will not work in China; and (3) leaders in China need to blend best Western practices with Chinese wisdom.

- It is naïve to think that best Western leadership practices can just be described and applied in China. Cultural differences between China and the West make some practices very difficult to implement in China.

- Many books on leadership written by Westerners assume that a close relationship between the leader and the followers is expected. This is not always the case in China, which has a high power-distance culture. The assumption that all Chinese leaders desire to be close to their followers is false.

- Empowering employees is a basic best Western leadership practice. In China, it needs to be done within the realities of a Confucianist hierarchical culture.

- Chinese and Western views of trust are very different. Chinese employees need more time than Westerners before they can trust someone.

- The Chinese tend to have less tolerance than Westerners for leaders who initiate change often.

- Westerners usually have their eyes on the ends, while Chinese leaders focus more on the means. While both cultures respect the need to have good means to justify their desired ends, there is a difference in the degree of focus, which may lead to workplace conflict between Westerners and Chinese.

Chapter 2

METHODOLOGY AND FORMAT OF THE BOOK

Methodology and Format of the Book

The book's content comes from three sources: (1) professional literature; (2) interviews with leaders in China; and (3) my own experience as a consultant, executive coach, and trainer in China.

Professional Literature. I personally reviewed all of the relevant Western literature. Ms. (Sally) Xue Gong conducted the Chinese literature review and produced English abstracts, which we then discussed in detail. I occasionally went to other Chinese experts when I still had questions about the meaning of some Chinese terms and concepts. The primary sources here were Ding Jingping, Shi Lan, and (Richard) Xu Yue. All the interviewees, along with descriptions of their backgrounds, are listed in Appendix 1.

Professional Interviews. Twenty interviews were conducted with current leaders in Chinese companies, as well as with experts in Chinese leadership or Chinese wisdom. Most of the interviewees are Chinese nationals, although they include a few foreigners who have extensive experience in managing and leading people in China. The interviewees were the primary sources of information for me on which Western practices work well in

China, which ones need to be modified, and which ones just do not fit within Chinese culture today. You will find anecdotes from the interviews throughout the text.

My Own Experience. As of this writing, I have lived and worked in China for more than nine years. I began as Managing Director for Greater China of human resources giant, Watson Wyatt. In this role, I learned firsthand what it meant to lead in China. I will share some of my successes and failures, as well as the various approaches I used to modify my style whenever I saw the need. I retired from Watson Wyatt in 2004 and began my own consulting firm, Calypso Consulting. This firm is devoted to improving the level of leadership in China—be the leader Chinese or foreign. In 2009 I joined Hewitt Associates as Chief Leadership Consultant for Greater China. My work involves executive coaching, leadership consulting, and leadership workshop delivery. While I am often referred to as an expert in this work, I still feel that this is as much a learning opportunity for me as it is for my clients.

How to Use This Book

Part I offers an understanding of business leadership in China. The *preface* and the *first chapter* describe why this book was written and how it was developed. This *second chapter* describes the book's methodology, as well as how best to use it. The *third chapter* provides an overview of leadership and leadership needs in China. Some of the themes introduced in that chapter will be examined in more detail in later chapters when we review them from the Chinese and Western perspectives. The second and third chapters also make reference to some of the key Western and Chinese texts on business leadership in China that provided a theoretical foundation for this book. The *fourth and fifth chapters* provide a detailed socio-cultural analysis of how managers who grew up in completely different cultures developed quite differently as leaders. Their practices, and the history and values that shape them, are indeed different. This leads to the *sixth chapter*, which describes those traits considered by current

Chinese leaders to be unique to China and not often found in Western leaders. *Chapter Seven* focuses on one prevailing characteristic of admired Chinese leaders; how they try to lead from the heart, rather than just from the brain. *Chapter Eight* provides a review of the key human resources (HR) trends in China, examining their similarities to and differences from trends in the West and how these underlie the approaches described in Part II of the book.

The *ninth through the nineteenth chapters* that make up Part II are perhaps the heart of the book. In these chapters, we identify the key features of business success in the West, such as decision-making, empowerment, employee motivation, and legality, and try to integrate these and other important business issues into a workable format for leaders in China.

Part III focuses on what we need to do next in order to improve business leadership in China. The *twentieth chapter* outlines what a comprehensive leadership program in China should look like. The *twenty-first chapter* provides a guideline for the Chinese manager, as well as the company, on how Chinese managers can progress from being a Chinese manager to a global leader. The *twenty-second chapter* contains concluding remarks and suggested next steps.

Each chapter concludes with an Executive Summary. The bulleted items in these summaries contain the main points of the chapter and can be read independently by the person who wants to get the gist of the book first and then go back for the details when time permits.

The appendices provide biographical details on the people who contributed to the development of the book, as well as a translation and a brief description of the key Chinese concepts that are referred to as being relevant to leadership in China. The bibliography is comprehensive and provides both English- and Chinese-language sources.

China is a huge country. Every location has its nuances of culture and behavior. In order not to get bogged down in small cultural nuances found in certain remote provinces, the focus in this book will be on the first-tier areas of China. These include

Beijing, Shanghai, Tianjin, Guangzhou, and Shenzhen. It is likely that the leadership issues described in this book are also found in the second-tier areas, where there are a significant number of businesses; these cities include Chengdu, Dalian, Hangzhou, Suzhou, Nanjing, and others. Trying to generalize beyond those areas to Yunnan, Tibet, and Xinjiang is perhaps too much of a stretch and requires further study.

Likewise, there are generational differences. Bin Gong, Regional HR Director for Bayer HealthCare, told me that he could make a good guess about a Chinese person's value system just by knowing his age.

> *"China has had so many campaigns and programs over the past 50 years. These programs have affected our own personal value systems. I am a 'qi qi ji' (七七级, class of '77). We were the first ones who entered college after the Cultural Revolution. If you gathered a group of 'qi qi ji,' you would find a very similar set of values. It would be very different from the 'ba ling hou' (八零后, those born after 1980). Westerners tend to group all Chinese into one culture, but actually we have many cultures here. A Westerner needs to understand this."*
>
> **Bin Gong**, *Regional HR Director, Asia Pacific, Bayer HealthCare, Hong Kong.*

It is a bold task for an American to write about life in China. China is a fascinating country and a place that I have referred to as home over the past several years. But the more I learn about this wonderful and complex country, the more I realize how little I really understand. Alas, how much of a foreigner I still remain. I do hope, however, that this modest book on only one subject in China—business leadership—can serve as another bridge between Chinese and Western people. The book is intended to benefit both foreigners who are trying to work effectively in China, as well as those Chinese who are attempting to merge all that they have absorbed from Chinese philosophy with the best Western practices in order to make them better leaders here. If this book can do that in some small way, then I am deeply humbled and exceedingly grateful.

Chapter Two Executive Summary

Methodology and Format of the Book

- Content for the book comes from literature review, professional interviews, and the author's experience as a leader in China.

- The book is divided into three parts. The first part provides an introduction to leadership in China and describes some significant cultural differences between China and the West. Among these differences are the key traits expected of Chinese leaders. As you will note, these are very different from what are typically found in lists of Western leadership traits.

- Part II provides detailed descriptions of business issues that may cause conflict between Westerners and Chinese. Several chapters in this part also offer suggestions on how to deal with those conflicts.

- Part III focuses on what China needs to do now in order to help improve its business leadership performance, and also suggests next steps for further study and discussion.

- The reader needs to understand that China is a huge country and there are geographical differences in culture. This can sometimes apply to leadership. However, the focus in this book will be on business leadership in the first-tier areas of China—Beijing, Shanghai, Tianjin, Guangzhou, and Shenzhen.

- Besides geographical distinctions, there are also huge differences in how people of different ages view and react to leadership.

- This book is written by a foreigner living in China. That, in itself, is a cause for humility. But the intention is to teach and to share with the expectation that what is written here will, in some small way, contribute to improving the level of business leadership in China.

Chapter 3

SPECIAL LEADERSHIP NEEDS IN CHINA

Why does China need leaders more than any other country? What is special about China that makes this a crisis, rather than just a normal business need?

There are two answers to these questions, one relating to demography and the other to culture. Demographically, China forfeited an entire generation of possible business leaders during the Cultural Revolution in the 1960s. People who would now be of an age to be in charge of firms spent many of their formative years in the countryside learning the agrarian way of life. Business as we know it today was shunned. While Westerners were sowing their oats in college and then landing their first jobs that would mark the beginning of their long business careers, their Chinese counterparts were toiling in the fields. When the Cultural Revolution ended, some of these people entered the workforce, but they entered into a planned economy where market forces played no part. There was no need to learn the things leaders need to know today in order to be successful. As a result, we now have an older workforce in China that was never groomed in a market economy.

Today, the younger generation in China dominates the workforce. It is estimated that Chinese employees are on average 10 years younger than their counterparts holding a comparable job in the West. Most people who are required to lead have no experience of leading and very little experience of being led. The situation is similar to the high-tech boom in Silicon Valley in the US in the late 1990s, when people in their mid-twenties were being asked to lead groups. It was difficult then in the US, and it is equally difficult today in China. This problem will be resolved in a few years as the population ages and the current crop of managers gains valuable experience. But until that happens, China will continue to have a leadership shortage.

The cultural issue is more complex and will not necessarily be resolved quickly. The basic tenets of life in China are so different from those in most Western countries. Many of the cultural practices the Chinese are taught as children are being turned upside down by some of the things Western business practices are asking them to do as leaders. Furthermore, the people who have attained leadership positions in their firms did so without the benefit of any of the practices that are so heavily touted in the Western business literature. This cultural issue underscores the purpose of this book.

Companies around the world are crying out for more and better leaders. A 2007 survey conducted by Deloitte Touche Tohmatsu and The Economist Intelligence Unit asked over 500 executives about their most significant people challenges. Over 76 percent indicated that the most critical people management issue relating to organizational success was leadership development and the leadership pipeline.[1] This is certainly true in China. The Hewitt Associates Best Employers survey for 2005 found that more than 70 percent of what they considered to be the "best companies" in China identified leadership as their primary talent need.[2]

In addition to this need is the economic impact of not having good leaders in place. A recent Watson Wyatt study found that companies with high trust and confidence in their senior leadership had a 108 percent total return to shareholders, compared to only 66 percent for companies where trust and confidence in their leaders was low. The same study found high positive correlations between employee commitment and market value.[3]

In survey after survey in China, companies are indicating that their leadership development programs are ineffective. An online survey by Hewitt Associates of 138 companies in China found that 73 percent of them saw their leadership programs as ineffective.[4]

Most of the companies surveyed admitted that leadership problems in their companies were affecting their business results. In 2005, Development Dimensions International (DDI) conducted a survey of tomorrow's global leaders. The survey found that nearly 25 percent of Chinese leaders in China were weak in the skills that were most critical for success in their roles. They broke down the skills needed into four general categories: getting results, relationship management, coaching and development, and managing performance. Respondents indicated each of these areas as weak.[5]

In another such survey, when companies were questioned about the specific problems with their leadership programs, they pointed to several: an over-emphasis on short-term operations; the lack of know-how and experience within the company to develop new leaders; a lack of talent internally; the unwillingness of some managers to allow people to take the time required for leadership development; and, related to the prior problem, the unwillingness of some managers to try something different.[6] Let us take a look at each of these impediments to developing leaders in China.

Impediments to Developing Leaders in China

Short-Term Focus. Every public company in the world has short-term worries. But in China, the preoccupation is greater than in most other places. Multinationals have bosses in other countries who often believe that China is a place to maximize profits today. Costs are still relatively low. The mindset is to squeeze the most from the stone now while it is still possible. Local firms have a different reason for the short-term focus—survival. Without the deep pockets of the multinationals, local firms must capitalize on whatever economies they can make today so that they will still be around tomorrow. This extreme short-term focus is very different from the recent past in China, when time was not an issue. Companies did only what they needed to do and continued to receive financial support from Beijing. But as the economy has changed from one based on planning to one based on market forces, all of this has changed. With such a short-term focus, whether you are a multinational or a local firm, long-term efforts such as leadership development often take a backseat.

Lack of Know-How and Experience. While all of the multinational firms in China have leadership development expertise in their home countries, few have adequately transferred that expertise to China. In the case of local firms, there never has been much experience of developing leaders through formal programs. As such, there are not enough people in China who know how to do this well. Therefore, leadership development often gets allocated to outside consultants, if it gets done at all. While the consultants can do a good job, it is not the same as having this built into the DNA of the corporate culture.

Lack of Talent Internally. Chinese employees are among the brightest and the most hardworking in the world. But they are so young! Many Chinese managers have only a few years of work experience before they are asked to lead people on the job. As noted above, Chinese managers are roughly 10 years younger than their counterparts in the West. Most have not even been mentored and yet, they are being required to lead others. While this is a short-term problem, there is a great need today for talent. Until these future leaders "grow up," there will continue to be a lack of internal leadership talent in China.

Giving People Time for Leadership Development. Time is of the essence in China. The pressure to get products and services out the door quickly, and to turn them into profit, is perhaps greater in China than in most countries. There is little patience to be found in foreign headquarters when it involves delays in deliveries from China. The name of the game is quick profit. Leadership development in China requires line managers to allow employees to leave the assembly line and participate in programs with a long-term focus, when the manager is already under pressure to achieve measurable short-term gains. It is not always an easy decision, and line managers often need to be convinced (or persuaded) to let their people participate in these programs. Suggestions for overcoming this barrier will be offered in a later chapter when we discuss what a great leadership program in China should look like.

Trying Something New and Different. The concept of doing things in new and different ways is attracting much discussion in China. The Chinese have a reputation for not being innovative enough to compete in a global economy. Yet, most Chinese leaders in government and business understand that they must do this, and they must do it now. In fact, some of the better universities have already begun to modify their teaching techniques to breed innovation rather than rote learning and repetition. But the reality is that most leaders in China did not get to their leadership positions by doing things differently. Rather, they got there by doing what they were supposed to do in a reliable way. Risks were limited to making modifications to existing procedures—not introducing entirely new ones. So, the process of identifying high-potential employees and sending them off to workshops designed to improve their leadership abilities is still relatively untested in China. While multinationals have plenty of experience with this practice in their home countries, Chinese firms are still on a steep learning curve. The trend is certainly moving in the direction of experimenting with leadership development, but skepticism about its usefulness remains.

So, while business in China is growing at lightning speed and the need for more and better leaders grows proportionately, there are more cultural barriers to developing these leaders than in the West. How can they be overcome?

Let us take a look at what some Chinese leaders and leadership experts see as special considerations for developing leaders in China.

Gao Yong of Career International addresses the first theme of this book—the need to improve the level of leadership in China. He indicates that, compared to the West, the short period during which China has been a part of the global market economy has not yet allowed it to develop its leaders properly.

> "Westerners have had a long time to develop their leaders. In China, we have only been at this for about 10 years. The process is going to take much longer. We need more time to have enough good leaders to run our companies. But for now, our existing managers will do the best they can by reading, observing, and gaining more education. Coaching can also help and we need to do it more."
>
> **Gao Yong**, President, Career International, Inc., Beijing, China.

Oftentimes, however, the home country bosses are unwilling to take the time necessary to develop the company's China leaders and will tend to rely on expatriates to do the job. While these imported leaders may indeed be experienced, in most cases, that experience was gained somewhere other than China. As Yi Min of Lenovo describes below, there is no guarantee that this formula will be successful in China.

> *"Until we can develop more Chinese leaders, we will need to continue to depend on foreigners. But for these foreigners to be successful here, they must understand Chinese culture and learn to incorporate the wisdom from this ancient culture into their business practices. Foreign leaders who just try to impose their Western practices here will be seen as arrogant and foolish and they will not succeed."*
>
> **Yi Min**, *Director of Global Leadership and Organization Development, Lenovo Group, Raleigh, North Carolina, United States.*

Yi Min's words succinctly describe the second and third themes of this book—namely, that we cannot expect the simple importation of best Western leadership practices to work in China without modification, and that the best leaders in China will successfully blend all of what they have learned about best leadership practices with relevant aspects of Chinese wisdom. As Yi Min indicates, leaders who cannot do this well will fail in China.

Ding Jingping of the Pan Pacific Management Institute echoes these themes and also offers an explanation for why many Chinese leaders are unwilling to invest too much time and money in leadership development programs in China. He also offers a note of caution about the leadership gap continuing to exist as long as the current crop of older leaders in China's businesses continues to rule.

> *"We still have a long way to go in China to develop enough leaders for our companies. Many of the people in charge grew up in the 'school of hard knocks' and are not so willing to allow their younger employees to have special development programs. It is okay to send people to*

> (*continued*)
>
> *training, but not much more. Many of these senior managers learned about leadership in the People's Liberation Army. The Army has a very different approach to developing leaders from what the current literature suggests. Until these people retire from their management roles, or are forced out in some other way, we will not be developing leaders as much as we need to."*
>
> **Ding Jingping**, *Senior Partner and Vice President, Pan Pacific Management Institute, Beijing, China.*

Ren Jianxin, President of China National Chemical Corp., China's (and perhaps the world's) largest domestic industrial-cleaning company, was quoted in the *McKinsey Quarterly* as saying: "When I was working as a farmer in Ganxu province during the Cultural Revolution, the hard life there taught me how to persistently pursue my goals. These lessons have carried me over into my business career."[7]

Li Dongsheng is CEO of the mammoth Chinese appliance maker, TCL, which began as a local Chinese firm. Li was quoted in an interview as saying that any problems he faces in the firm are small compared to what he had to face during the Cultural Revolution, when he worked in the rice paddies. "If ever I hit problems along the way, I think: 'This is nothing like what I faced down on the farm.'"[8]

Xu Fang is head of TCL's Institute of Leadership Development. She offers cautious optimism about how the leadership level in China is gradually improving. While I believe she would agree with the general sentiment expressed by Dr. Ding, she comments that TCL is making gradual improvements in its leadership development, and is confident that this can be applied elsewhere in China.

> *"At TCL, we formed an Institute of Leadership Development. We are trying to develop our own leaders rather than just hire leaders from outside. We need our most senior people to understand the importance*
>
> (*continued*)

(continued)

of developing others. This is a new concept for many of our existing leaders. Many of them are very strong personalities who grew into their positions by working very hard and very long. The idea that we would actually help develop others into leadership positions still needs to be proven to some of these existing leaders. But little by little, it is working and I am optimistic that we will soon have a culture of leadership development that resembles that of Western firms."

Xu Fang, *Vice President, TCL Institute of Leadership Development, TCL Corporation, Huizhou, China.*

This book's three major themes were developed following my discussions with these experts. They were not hypotheses that I generated and then sought to prove. These are issues strongly emphasized by current Chinese leaders. For Chinese business to improve, these issues need to be addressed and resolved without delay.

Can the Chinese Business Leadership Gap be Narrowed?

Where do we go from here? How can China increase the rate of developing leaders in order to help close the gap between supply and demand? The answer needs to be owned, at least partially, by those people who are entrusted with managing and leading in China today.

Foreigners operating in China need to learn as much about Chinese culture as they can, so that they can integrate that knowledge with the Western practices they are already comfortable with. They also need to educate their home offices about the differences they encounter. It is not sufficient just to say, "Things are very different here." Home country executives have been hearing this comment for years and are frustrated by it. We need to demonstrate with real examples how applying best Western practices without significant modification just does not work in China.

Here is one such example I have personally observed. A Western-educated CEO in China wanted to empower his employees. He held regular meetings with his managers and their subordinates and challenged them to fix certain corporate problems. The feedback from the employees was that the CEO was "weak." Since he could not figure out how to solve corporate problems, he passed them on to the employees who were looking to him for solutions, not more responsibility.

Another example relates to a US manufacturing company with a large plant in northeast China. The company is very safety-conscious and implemented several rules and regulations aimed at protecting its employees. The plant manager was very emphatic about these rules and insisted that the supervisors enforce them rigorously. But the plant employees thought the rules were ridiculous and objected strongly to following them. "Why can't I use my cell phone when walking around?" "Wearing a helmet at all times in the plant is uncomfortable and unnecessary." "Not letting me run causes me not to get things done as quickly as I could otherwise. Running is not a problem for me. I have been running for years."

A third example comes from my own experience. My firm was conducting a consulting project with a well-known Chinese high-tech firm fairly smoothly. The project was about one-third done when the management changed and the person who had been the client sponsor left the firm. The replacement person was not interested in the project and was unwilling to continue it. More importantly, she was unwilling to pay for the work that had already been done. After nine months of tedious negotiation, a compromise was eventually reached. But the wounds between the two firms never healed.

These are just three of the countless examples of challenges managers in China face. Even the best Western managers would face these difficulties in China and need to learn new ways of leading if they are to get results.

For local Chinese leaders, the challenge is to be more open to the development of the best and the brightest in the firm. You may be able to teach some people to swim by throwing them in the water and letting them fend for themselves, but you can be much more efficient if you give them swimming lessons. The same goes for business leadership. If we just assume that the best leaders will figure it out on their own, we are wasting valuable time and valuable human resources. An investment in future leaders is an investment in the company that will pay huge dividends. It is not a choice. Chinese companies cannot afford to wait for leaders to develop naturally. If the current Chinese leaders take this approach, they will surely lose out to their competitors who will simply recruit this pool of valuable talent and make them leaders in their companies.

If foreign leaders are more understanding of Chinese ways, and if Chinese leaders are more open to using Western leadership development practices, it will go a long way toward meeting the leadership challenges that China offers.

Notes

1   Deloitte Touche Tohmatsu and The Economist Intelligence Unit, *Aligned at the Top* (Deloitte Development LLC, 2007), p. 6.
2   Hewitt Associates, *Best Employers Survey*, 2005.
3   Bruce N. Pfau and Ira T. Kay, *The Human Capital Edge* (New York: McGraw-Hill, 2002), p. 204.
4   Hewitt Associates, *Leadership Development in China: Learning from Top Asian Companies* (Internet report) (Lincolnshire, IL: December 2003).
5   Paul R. Bernthal, Jason Bondra, and Wei Wang, *Leadership in China* (Pittsburgh, PA: Development Decisions International, 2005).
6   Hewitt Associates, *Leadership Development in China: Learning from Top Asian Companies, op. cit.*, p. 2.
7   Tomas Koch and Oliver Ramsbottom, "A Growth Strategy for a Chinese State-Owned Enterprise," *McKinsey Quarterly*, July 2008, p. 1.
8   Matthew Forney, Time Magazine.com, December 17, 2004, p. 1.

Chapter Three Executive Summary

Special Leadership Needs in China

- One reason that China has special leadership needs is demographic. An entire generation of potential business leaders languished during the Cultural Revolution. Only a small percentage of that generation became business leaders. The result is a relatively young work population compared to that in the West. This will change over time as the population ages, but in the meantime, there will be a shortage in the talent pool.

- Another reason for China's inability to quickly develop leaders is cultural. Many of today's senior managers in China got to their positions through personal struggle. They see this as the best way to get ahead and are not keen on developing special programs to develop new leaders.

- Multiple surveys show a shortage of Chinese leaders when compared to the need. Many surveys also show China's leadership development programs to be ineffective. More importantly, they indicate the enormous financial loss to China because of its inability to meet its leadership needs.

- Several barriers exist that impede the rapid development of China's leaders. These include: a short-term focus on business results at the expense of long-term needs such as leadership development; lack of know-how and experience by those in China who are charged with designing and implementing leadership development programs; a lack of talent internally, caused by the relative youthfulness of people placed in management positions; an unwillingness to give people time off the line to participate in leadership programs; and a general discomfort on the part of current senior executives about trying something new and different, such as a leadership development program.

- To overcome these barriers, solutions need to come both from foreigners who are working in Chinese leadership programs now, and from local Chinese who also hold these positions. Foreigners need to acknowledge their need to become more understanding of Chinese culture in order to modify the current best Western leadership practices that they often take for granted as valuable. Locals need to be more open to the Western practices of giving employees time off to learn to become better leaders.

Chapter 4

PHILOSOPHICAL AND CULTURAL FOUNDATIONS OF WESTERN LEADERSHIP

Westerners cherish their individual freedom and liberty and "perceived" equality. Mottos, national anthems, and government proclamations are constant reminders of this. While some may argue that these freedoms and other cherished values are really myths, the majority of Westerners believe they are their foundation.

Let us examine some of the primary things Westerners teach their children in the hope that they will become exemplary adults.

Equality

One of my first "startling" experiences in China was a visit to a client's company headquarters in Jinan. I was being given a tour of the facility by the CEO. As we entered each new space, the employees would immediately stand at attention until we left the area. Some employees saluted. It reminded me of my military days. I soon learned that this was an exceptional situation—a state-owned enterprise that was run by a retired army general. Nevertheless, the point was well made. This was so different from what I was used to. In the US, I worked for one high-tech company that was very egalitarian. Everyone was on a first-name basis. The CEO drove his own car and had to park in the employee lot, just like everyone else. It was first-come, first-served. We all ate in the same dining room. While both of these examples are extreme, the roots of egalitarianism in the West versus hierarchical roles in China are clear.

I also remember the horror of my Chinese staff when I asked for a smaller office and a smaller car than they thought I should have. I was just being frugal and felt that the status that came from having a big office and a big car was no longer important in my own life and should not be a model for the firm. In China, however, certain things are expected of a CEO. In the eyes of my employees, by seeking a smaller office and car, I was belittling the firm's value in the eyes of the Chinese market. This seemingly benign stance taken by many Western leaders can be a source of conflict between them and their Chinese staff.

Independence

Many Western books on parenting emphasize that the primary goal of a parent is to teach their children to be independent of them. The sooner their children can become self-reliant and live on their own, the better one would judge their parenting success. In the West today, as many older children are forced, for economic or social reasons, to return to the parental nest, a sense of failure is felt by both the parents and the children. This return to the nest must be seen as temporary. Otherwise, society will deem this child a failure who was unable to make it on his or her own.

Perhaps America typifies this trait more than other Western countries. There are so many success stories of people who "did it on their own." People in the West are often reluctant to admit that others may have had a hand in their success. They much prefer to minimize the importance of any outside help they may have received. While it is fine to identify a mentor or another who was influential in developing one's thinking, it is always the individual who was smart enough to "use" others to achieve his or her success.

Let us not forget that the US was formed with a document entitled the Declaration of Independence. American soldiers are willing to die to help preserve the right of Americans to be unique.

But sometimes, this Western independence is viewed negatively in China.

> *"Westerners can be seen as show-offs. Even though their intent is just to demonstrate their independence, they can be seen as taking credit for something they did not do. We Chinese believe that what we do is usually the result of the group, not of any one individual. If the leader tries to take credit, there will be resentment and the leader may be seen as arrogant. Actually, we want just the opposite from our leaders. We want them to be 'di diao' (低调, low-key)."*
>
> **Kelly Wang**, *Founder and Director, GW Technologies Co., Ltd., Beijing, China.*

One long-time Western leader in China, Jim Leininger of Watson Wyatt, indicates how he has had to be careful in China of how his ideas on independence are viewed by his Chinese employees. He believes that his desire to help employees become independent has sometimes been confused with selfishness.

> *"I had an experience early in my career in China where what I considered to be independence was perceived by an employee as a selfish inner focus that was even anti-family. I was asking the employee to take on an assignment in a distant city that required a great deal of travel. While I believed that this assignment was good for the employee's career and would help her learn to work independently, she felt that I was putting the needs of the company above the needs of her family. I learned from this experience to try to find a balance between what I perceived as an employee's need to be independent and their own perception of what was important to them."*
>
> **Jim Leininger**, *General Manager, Watson Wyatt Worldwide, Beijing, China.*

Individualism

Closely related to independence is individualism. Westerners are taught from a very early age to develop all the necessary skills to make it on their own. Joseph Campbell makes this very clear. "The best part of Western tradition has included a recognition of and respect for the individual. The function of the society is to cultivate the individual. It is not the function of the individual to support society."[1]

Your parents and teachers make it clear that your individualism is special. It is more important than the group. You own things that are yours. Sharing becomes your prerogative. While children are taught to share, the implication is that it is your individual decision to share. Property can be owned and is private. Only you can give permission to share it or to make it public.

> *"China is not interested in building strong individuals—we had that in our history. We had kings and we had Mao. By acting strong, they actually lowered themselves. Rather, we prefer humility. We prefer our leaders to be more silent than Western leaders try to be."*
>
> **Guo Xin**, *Managing Director, Greater China, Mercer Consulting, Beijing, China.*

When Westerners rely too much on their individualism, their behavior is sometimes seen as that of a show-off. One Chinese writer on leadership referred to American leaders as peacocks because of their outward appearance of grandeur while their inner self is comparatively weak.[2] Chinese leaders, as Kelly Wang noted, prefer to be low-key (低调, *di diao*) whenever possible.

Freedom

In the US Constitution, the Bill of Rights lists the basic freedoms of every person. These rights form the foundation of most court cases. When these freedoms are threatened, Westerners (and Americans, in particular) are very vocal and will fight until the threat is removed. When Westerners go to war, it is almost always to defend their idea of "freedom." As mentioned earlier, the US state of New Hampshire has the motto, "Live Free or Die." Patrick Henry, an important historical figure in the American War of Independence against Britain, is famous for his statement, "Give me liberty or give me death." Westerners view dictatorial leaders as despicable because they are seen to restrict individual freedoms.

Freedom is often a source of great conflict in Western nations. Lawyers are always arguing in court to determine which freedom is more important. Do I have the right to go to a certain restaurant, or does the restaurant owner have the right to exclude me? The answers to these questions are often not very clear. Western leaders from different points on the political spectrum may have very different views on how to interpret what is meant by "freedom." One often must decide on the freedom of the individual versus the freedom of the company. Another example of this conflict is flag burning. In many Western countries, a citizen is free to publicly burn or destroy his or her country's flag. While the practice is generally abhorred by most other citizens, it is still permitted by law because it is considered one's right to have freedom of expression. In China, such an act would lead to a person being jailed and severely punished.

What is also important for the Chinese person to understand about Western views on freedom is that, while the concept is extremely important, its application is dependent on the person's own views on which aspects of freedom are most important.

It should be pointed out that the Chinese also revere freedom. But unlike in the West, it is not an individualistic freedom to do whatever one wishes. Rather, it is freedom that comes from the government which allows people to say and do things that are not harmful to the central good of the country. Of course, the Chinese government determines what that central good is. Actually, most Westerners are surprised by just how much freedom the Chinese have. The big difference is in how it is controlled. Someone once joked that there was absolute freedom in China as long as you did not do one of three things: (1) talk about a free Taiwan; (2) talk about a free Dalai Lama; or (3) talk about a free Falun Gong (or any other group that criticizes China).

Risk-Taking

"Nothing ventured, nothing gained." "You will never know unless you try." "Go for it!" These are just a few of the often-repeated mantras in the West about taking a risk. People who always take the safe path are considered boring and conventional and are not sought out by leading-edge firms.

Conversely, the Chinese are often accused of not being as willing to take risks as their Western counterparts. I am not sure this is true. But I have often observed very severe penalties being imposed on Chinese workers who make mistakes. In the early days of business in China, we heard stories of errant workers being made to stand in a corner wearing a dunce cap so that everyone would know they had made a mistake. Such forms of punishment do not encourage one to take risks. In fact, there is a Chinese saying, *Tao guang yang hui* (稻光养晦), which means one should hide one's capabilities in order to prevent others from seeing a possible error. Another famous saying, *Qiang da chu tou niao* (枪打出头鸟), means the first bird out gets shot. In other words, the more you can hide your capabilities and intentions, the safer you will be.

While nearly every Chinese firm today wants people to take risks and encourages them to do so, there is still this deep-seated cultural fear that sometimes undermines people's desire to do so. This is very different in the West, where people are taught from an early age to be always willing to try something new.

Trust in Others

This is a basic tenet that Western children are taught from a very early age. While the new age of terrorism has modified this level of trust, there is still a sense in the West that people are generally trustworthy. Western leaders usually begin their assignments with a given trust of their workforce. They continue this way unless they are given cause to think differently. Workers are also likely to trust their leaders, until they give them a reason to question that trust.

Nandani Lynton of Thunderbird University, an expert on Chinese business practices, has described the difference between the "personal trust" required in China, and the "formal trust" that is fostered in Western companies. Formal trust allows you to trust a stranger who works in the company, or even someone who works for another respected firm. The assumption is that these others share the same business goals and values as oneself. Lynton comments that if Chinese firms cannot encourage formal trust, they will have a difficult time empowering others and this, in turn, could slow down their global expansion efforts.[2]

Honesty

There is a fable in the US about George Washington and a cherry tree. George Washington was the first President of the United States. According to the fable, when George was six years old, he was given a hatchet as a present. He was very fond of this tool, and would use it to chop at everything he could find. One day, when he was playing in the garden with his hatchet, he saw a young cherry tree. He used his hatchet on the tree and it soon died. He had not intended to kill the tree, and he knew that his father would be very angry about it, so he kept quiet about what he had done. A few days later, his father discovered that the tree had been destroyed. As expected, he was very angry and wanted to know what had happened. When he saw George with his hatchet, he asked: "Do you know who chopped down my cherry tree?"

George began to cry and said: "Father, I cannot tell a lie. It was I who cut down the tree." His father replied: "My son, that you should tell the truth is much more important to me than any tree. Although I loved that tree, I love your honesty more and I forgive you."

Every American child is told this story in elementary school to teach them the value of always telling the truth.

Unfortunately, not every Westerner is as truthful as George Washington was in this story. But honesty is a fundamental value in Western culture. This is why Westerners who come to China to do business are often puzzled by what they see as a "dishonest" business culture.

Summary

Westerners, like people everywhere, are taught from a very early age what their parents and forefathers believe are the essential values that will make them better people in the world. The seven values described in this chapter—equality, independence, individualism, freedom, risk-taking, trust in others, and honesty—are fundamental to most Western countries' culture. But Western leaders doing business in China must understand that these values may be viewed quite differently there and may not, at the outset, be considered as important as Westerners have been taught to believe. Likewise, Chinese leaders who are leading or working with Westerners need to appreciate the importance that Westerners place on these values. Only with this mutual understanding will Westerners and Chinese be able to work together cooperatively.

In the next chapter, we will view the world from the perspective of the Chinese leader.

Notes

1   Joseph Campbell, *The Power of Myth* (New York: Anchor Books, 1991), p. 239.
2   Shao Kun Mo, *Great Leadership* (Beijing: Oriental Press, 2006), p. 102.
3   Nandani Lynton, "Challenges for the Chinese Executive," *Thunderbird*, Fall 2006, p. 40.

Chapter Four Executive Summary

Philosophical and Cultural Foundations of Western Leadership

- Westerners cherish many values. Most Westerners believe these values are universally cherished in the same way—and, if not, they should be. This cultural insensitivity causes many Western leaders to fail in China, where the value system is quite different from that in the West.

- People in the West usually believe that equality is an important value in China. In fact, there is a hierarchy in business and other organizations that gives the leader a much higher status within the firm than in most Western cultures. This inequality is often surprising to Westerners when they first come to China. Western leaders need to learn how to cope with this expectation of status versus the egalitarianism that is more common in Western cultures.

- The Chinese sometimes see Western independence as "showiness." Some Chinese have referred to the typical Westerner as a peacock—flashy and beautiful to look at, but without much strength or substance. Standing alone, as independence often requires, is anathema to Chinese thinking.

- Western individualism is occasionally viewed as arrogance in China. Westerners take pride in their personal achievements. This sometimes causes a Western leader to take credit for something that the Chinese team believes is a team effort. Western leaders need to be very careful to acknowledge the value of their team in all their public and private presentations.

- Freedom is a value that is cherished in both China and the West. But its meaning in China is quite different from in the West, where freedom is essentially an individual value. In China, freedom is more a value of the country. People in China are free to behave as they wish, as long as they do not violate the laws, rules, and norms of the country. While American law gives a citizen the freedom to burn the American flag, this would be viewed in China as a violation of the freedom of the people, and any perpetrator would therefore be severely punished.

(continued)

(continued)

- Westerners are taught from an early age to take risks. There are many sayings and mottos that encourage this. In China, while companies today are trying to encourage this behavior more and more, there is still a tendency to try and avoid making a mistake for fear of punishment. In fact, in early history, the punishment for failure was often death. This kind of "fear culture" does not encourage innovativeness and risk-taking. Western leaders need to be aware of this in their handling of Chinese employees and encourage the risk-taking they require, reinforcing that the consequence of failure by trying is a new learning process, not a cause for punishment.

- One needs to earn others' trust in China. There have been too many cases of broken trust over the years to allow many Chinese to enter a new situation with the kind of open arms that are often found in Western transactions. But once the trust is earned, it is very strong. So, Western leaders need to learn patience in gaining trust. Likewise, Chinese, while continuing to be cautious, should understand that many Westerners enter a deliberation openly and with an expectation of trust. Neither party should expect to take unfair advantage of this.

- Westerners respect and expect honesty in their dealings with others. This is not to say that all Westerners are honest. We know that this is not the case. Nevertheless, we cannot deny the importance of this value to Westerners, at least in the ideal state. When dishonesty is prevalent in a business culture, as many Westerners believe to be the case in China, it becomes very difficult for them to do business. They are torn between fearing being taken advantage of because they will be honest and their competitor may not be, and choosing not to be honest themselves in order to level the playing field. Neither choice is workable in China.

Chapter 5

PHILOSOPHICAL AND CULTURAL FOUNDATIONS OF CHINESE LEADERSHIP

It is folly to generalize too much about Chinese culture and philosophy. China is a huge country with significant geographically based differences in how its people perceive the world. People who were born and raised in Tibet are very different from those raised in Beijing. People in Xinjiang are primarily Muslim and their cultural roots differ from those of the Han Chinese. In the northeast, there is a strong Russian influence. In the southeast, especially in Guangdong province, the commercial influence of Hong Kong is strongly felt. A cultural anthropologist could go on and on about these numerous distinctions in China.

But for our purposes, as we focus on business leadership, we will look only at those parts of the country where large corporations are based. In cities such as Shanghai, Beijing, Tianjin, Shenzhen, and Guangzhou, the leadership characteristics are quite similar. Of course, individual leaders will exhibit variations derived from their place of origin, but these differences are of less importance to us than the much broader philosophical and cultural underpinnings. These include the teachings found in Confucianism, Buddhism, and Daoism. They are also found in the words of well-known Chinese writers such as Sun Zi and leaders such as Sun Yat Sen, Deng Xiaoping, and Mao Zedong.

Additionally, people from different generations also think differently about business, and about how leaders should lead. Older leaders in China are typically less influenced by best Western practices than are younger ones. According to Gao Yong, President of Career International in Beijing, many older leaders have not had much opportunity to study Western leadership.

> *"When many of our current leaders in China were studying in college, there was not much in the way of Western practices to learn about. Unlike the West, where there is a fairly long history of professional business and leadership, China is pretty new at this. So, many of our leaders rely on what they know from ancient Chinese wisdom and also, in many cases, from the teachings of Mao. Many Chinese leaders like to read the words of Mao because they grew up with his teachings. There is a big connection between business and Communist leadership in China."*
>
> **Gao Yong**, *President, Career International, Inc., Beijing, China.*

As the themes of this book make clear, however, simply studying and applying best Western leadership practices won't make one a better leader in China. It is necessary to combine that knowledge with a cultural understanding of how things work in China, in order to make the Western leadership practices viable.

There are countless tomes describing the intricacies of these cultural underpinnings. Interested readers may want to take a look at the bibliography at the end of this book, especially the works by Chan,[1] Ebrey,[2] Buswell,[3] Wright,[4] and Becker.[5] Let us examine some of these roots of Chinese wisdom and see how they may relate to current business leadership.

Confucianism

Even though there were attempts to eliminate Confucian thinking in China during the Cultural Revolution, they were never fully successful. Today, Confucian thinking has had a resurgence and is a very important part of the Chinese persona. The Confucian concept of leading a virtuous life and adhering to the performance of one's duties pervades the Chinese mind. The three main Confucian principles—*ren* (仁, humaneness and love of one's fellow men), *yi* (义, morality and uprightness), and *li* (礼, rites and ritual propriety)—are cornerstones for how to live one's life. They are complemented by the five pairs of social roles that are understood by all Chinese people: between father and son; between the ruler and the subject; between the older and the younger; between husband and wife; and between friends. While these guidelines are not always followed as closely as they were intended when described by Confucius (and his most famous disciple, Mencius), they are still considered to indicate the proper way to behave in most social situations.

Xu Fang, Vice President of the TCL Institute of Leadership Development, explains the link she sees between Confucianism and current Chinese leadership.

"Most of my leadership ideas come from Confucianism. Even though it is mostly focused on how to govern the State, it should also influence business leaders. The Cultural Revolution destroyed much of this, but it still prevailed. The Confucian Doctrine of Humanity should be the core of a leader's ideology—bring peace and happiness to the entire population of the company. Great company leaders have a deep belief in this, but there is a difference between such a person and a typical businessman. These Confucian guidelines are not always easy to follow in business, but they should be what leaders aspire to do."

Xu Fang, *Vice President, TCL Institute of Leadership Development, TCL Corporation, Huizhou, China.*

Xu Fang is a very bright and well-informed expert on leadership in China. But note that she refers to "Confucianism" as the focus of her ideas on leadership—not one of the numerous Western books on leadership that she has read. This comment underscores the third theme of this book: that one needs to integrate best Western practices with Chinese wisdom in order to succeed as a leader in China.

Relationships are very important in Confucianism. The quote at the beginning of this chapter implies that everyone needs to understand their place in society. This is particularly important when we think about leadership. As noted in an earlier chapter, most Western leadership practices are based on the desire for a strong (sometimes collegial) relationship between the leader and his or her followers. But in Chinese society, especially as we consider Confucianism, there is a clearly defined distance in this relationship. Any attempts to narrow this distance (such as through the empowerment of employees) can cause conflict and discomfort. In a later chapter, we will discuss how a leader in China might deal with this potential conflict.

Another very important and relevant concept in Confucianism is that of the *jun zi* (君子, gentleman). Again, Xu Fang explains how this concept applies to Chinese leadership.

> *"In China, we expect our leaders to be 'jun zi' (君子). This means that they are kind and benevolent. They should be humble, tolerant, patient, patriotic, and have a sincere desire for corporate harmony. Others should also see them as people who greatly respect their own families and those of the employees. It disappoints me greatly to say that we do not always see this kind of behavior from our leaders. But it is still ingrained in all of us Chinese and we respect leaders who are truly 'jun zi'."*
>
> **Xu Fang**, *Vice President, TCL Institute of Leadership Development, TCL Corporation, Huizhou, China.*

It is interesting to note Xu Fang's use of the word "patriotic." We find this mentioned often in China in relation to desirable leadership qualities. It is even mentioned in the next chapter as a unique Chinese leadership trait. This tie-in between leading a business and expressing one's love for one's country is a very important Chinese phenomenon that is often not found in the West. It may partially explain the continued rift between Chinese and Westerners in business, as in most cases, the Westerner's main purpose in being in China is to achieve successful outcomes for his or her company. The Chinese leader and employees may, in fact, be looking to achieve successful outcomes for China as well.

Ren Binyan, Vice President of Alcoa China, gives an example of how a Chinese person might combine the two Confucian concepts of the relationship and be a gentleman.

"A Chinese employee would try to help his superior if he thinks the superior is acting incorrectly. This is related to the Confucian teaching that says that the inferior in the relationship must give advice to his superior if the superior is taking the wrong course of action. But if the leader objects to the assistance, then the junior person will back away and only return to help if asked by the senior. This is related to the Confucian teaching of being a gentleman and not offering something that is not desired."

Ren Binyan, *Vice President, Alcoa (China), Investment Company, Ltd., Beijing, China.*

This kind of Confucian guidance is still valued by many Chinese business leaders, especially those of the older generation. It is another reason Chinese employees sometimes look down on their Western business leaders, who they feel don't have the benefit of such ancient forms of guidance.

There is currently a resurgence of Confucianism in China. Many people are paying to attend lectures and take courses on this ancient philosophy. Universities are offering adult education courses on Confucianism and they are very well received. Chinese of all ages, especially those born after the Cultural Revolution, are keen to learn about Confucianism, as they believe it is an important missing part of their cultural upbringing.

Daoism

The two most commonly quoted ancient masters of Daoism are Zhuang Zi (庄子) and Lao Zi (老子). (They are more commonly known in the West as Chuang-tzu and Lao-tzu.) *Dao* (道) can be translated as "the Way." It refers to the natural flow of things in the world. One of my American colleagues who has lived in Beijing for many years jokingly remarks that to drive a car in China, one needs to be a Daoist. His comment refers to the seemingly chaotic flow of traffic that includes buses, trucks, cars, motorcycles, bicycles, and pedestrians—all seeming to be orchestrated by some higher power and not directed by any particular human traffic law.

Daoism is quite mystical and does not provide the kind of practical instructions that we find in Confucianism. The original Daoists, by choice, did not participate in government or commerce and rejected many of the Confucian concepts. Nevertheless, we can still see the influence of Daoism in modern China. For example, the concept of *yin* (阴) and *yang* (阳)—the balance of opposites—comes from Daoism. While this concept is usually disregarded in the linear-thinking West, it is quite a common consideration in China. For example, a Chinese leader will think about all sides of an issue before making a decision, in the hope of achieving outcomes that are harmonious and balanced; while a typical Western leader may consider it more important to be seen to be decisive and focused.

Gao Yong alludes to this in his statement about a common difference in the way Chinese and Westerners manage their employee relationships.

> *"The Western approach is pretty simple. You have key performance indicators (KPIs) that guide you. If employees meet their KPIs, they get rewarded. If not, they do not get rewarded. If they miss by too much, they may even get fired. It is a very focused and linear approach. The Chinese*

(continued)

leader is much more patient—friendship comes first. We can easily copy the Western reward system but we do much more. We cherish the relationships and harmony among our employees. There are lots of dinners, parties, and late-night drinking that involve informal communications on non-business topics such as family issues. We believe that this is the only way to lead people. We don't lead from the top, but from the middle."

Gao Yong, *President, Career International, Inc., Beijing, China.*

This is a very Daoist approach. It implies the need to have a holistic relationship with employees, which is not the typical Western approach to responding to problems and issues. It often takes Western leaders and their Chinese employees some time before they would both be comfortable with the kind of relationship described by Gao Yong.

Daoism also implies that leaders should be low-key in their attitudes and in their desire for position.

"We Chinese have a kind of mantra for leaders. It is 'wu wei er zhi' (无为而治). It means governing by doing nothing. The strong leader avoids subjecting subordinates to their way of thinking. Rather, they try to provide the environment where the subordinates do what they think is the right way."

Guo Xin, *Managing Director, Greater China, Mercer Consulting, Beijing, China.*

One would not typically expect this type of *laissez-faire* leadership from a Westerner. A Western leader in China, schooled in the ways of Western management, will typically be quite aggressive in leading others. Forming opinions and articulately espousing them is seen in the West as a critical success factor in leadership. But doing so in China may actually lead to a poor response from Chinese employees, who expect their leaders to be strong but low-key. In China, you display your strength with action. Overly aggressive words are seen as a sign that the leader may be unsure of his or her abilities and is using words to bolster his or her confidence.

So, unlike Confucianism, where there are countless statements attributed to Confucius's teachings that can be applied to business leadership, Daoism is more of a metaphysical experience that many Chinese have subsumed, simply by living and growing up in China. Westerners, unless they have undergone some form of metaphysical study, would most likely not have this kind of internal mechanism that may guide them in their thinking.

Buddhism

Like Daoism, Buddhism is metaphysical and is also quite evident in Chinese culture. All religions were suppressed during the Cultural Revolution, yet most survived somehow. Buddhism, especially with its strong ties to Tibet, was especially a problem. Today, China is much more liberal and many people openly practice Buddhism. The effect of Buddhism is to guide people to be reflective in all that they do. It teaches people to be honest, compassionate, and peaceful. It also teaches that one must have a peaceful mind and, through meditation, detach oneself from the physical world as much as possible.

Ruby Chen, Director of the McKinsey Leadership Institute in China, was raised in Taiwan. As a child, she was taught to take time out from her other activities three times each day for reflection and self-awareness.

> *"We were taught as children to take time out of a day to be self-reflective and to think about how our own behavior is influencing the world around us. It is very much this inner focus that I think is the basic difference between Chinese and Westerners. The latter are much more focused on the external and extroverted. We are, for the most part, introverts and rely on our inner self for many decisions. I ask myself before I ask others. For sure this is less evident today, especially in the big cities more than in the outer provinces, but it is still very much a part of our culture."*
>
> **Ruby Chen**, *Director of McKinsey Leadership Institute in China, Beijing, China.*

The concept of *wu* (悟), which is discussed at great length in the next chapter, is also derived from Buddhism. It is a very important trait in China and perhaps one of the defining differences between the Eastern and Western thinking processes. There is no one word in English that precisely translates this concept. It implies a very deep understanding of something, and can only come about by focusing inward and using all of one's senses to comprehend it.

> *"The noun form of 'wu' is 'wu xing' (悟醒). Many Chinese use this concept to describe strong insight, deep understanding, and thorough comprehension. It is a competency of good Chinese managers. Also, sometimes a Chinese manager will expect this ability from their employees. A typical Chinese manager may not give too clear directions for fear of making the employee think the manager does not trust their ability. So, to be a good subordinate, a key competency is to be able to use your 'wu' (悟) to guess the boss's meaning."*
>
> **Gao Yong**, President, Career International, Inc., Beijing, China.

Gao Yong's explanation tells us a lot about Chinese relationships. Westerners, especially Americans, tend to be very direct in their discussions with others. The Chinese, according to Gao, are much less so. For a variety of reasons that we will discuss later, the Chinese leader is often challenged to use *wu* to understand the world around him. In turn, he also expects his employees to use this same skill to understand his deepest meanings. This concept is alien to most Westerners! It may also cause them to question the integrity, or perhaps the confidence, of the Chinese leader in not being forthcoming with information. However, in many companies, especially SOEs, Chinese employees expect this uncertainty. In fact, they sometimes will look askance at the Western leader who offers a more straightforward form of communication. "How can my Western leader be so sure of this?" they may wonder. "Is there no room for doubt? Does my Western leader not see the other possibilities?"

Yi Min of Lenovo also talks about *wu*.

> *"'Wu xing' is a Buddhist concept that is not really teachable. It comes from exposure and wisdom. In leadership, we also use the term 'wu xing de ling dao' (*悟醒的领导*), which means a leader with very thorough insight. Good leaders in any country have this, but Chinese 'wu' is more complicated. It is derived from an inner understanding that comes from reflection."*
>
> **Yi Min**, *Director of Global Leadership and Organization Development, Lenovo Group, Raleigh, North Carolina, United States.*

Some have argued that this kind of holistic thinking also comes from the Chinese pictographic language, which is very different from the Roman alphabet used in Western countries. A picture tells a story that is often open to different interpretations. To read Chinese, a person needs to understand the context in which the characters are presented. In a Chinese conversation, there is often a back-and-forth discussion between speakers to clarify the meaning. Western words are more precise in their meaning and often less reliant on context. So, there is less need for *wu* in Western understanding.

Sun Zi

Beyond the major religions such as Confucianism, Daoism, and Buddhism, Chinese leadership culture also has its underpinnings in the writings of well-known thinkers not affiliated with any of these schools of thought. One such writer was Sun Zi, world-renowned author of *The Art of War* (孙子兵法).[6] Many of Sun's teachings, although aimed specifically at helping generals to win battles and wars, are also commonly used in business settings around strategy and leadership. Here is one example that can be applied to leadership.

> *"(T)he skillful leader subdues the enemy's troops without any fighting; he captures their cities without laying siege to them; he overthrows their kingdom without lengthy operations in the field."* (Sun Zi)

The leadership implication is that the great leader will use insight to figure out how to win. He will use the least necessary amount of resources to do this. He will succeed through a combination of clever maneuvering and patience.

Here is another example that teaches business leaders to have their companies prepared for any possible situation in the market.

> *"The Art of War (孙子兵法) teaches us to rely not on the likelihood of the enemy's not coming, but on our own readiness to receive him; not on the chance of his not attacking, but rather on the fact that we have made our position unassailable." (Sun Zi)*

All new leaders in China should read this readily available and brief treatise on warfare and try to understand its relationship to business. You can be sure that every Chinese leader will already have done so.

Other Cultural Influences

Many of China's past leaders, such as Sun Yat Sen, Mao Zedong, and Deng Xiaoping, are often quoted in management books. Sun Yat Sen often talked about being open to outside ideas. Mao's *Little Red Book* is owned and quoted by most Chinese, despite the fact that he is also often derided in China. Deng Xiaoping gave the Chinese people "permission" to get rich and to do so in whatever ways that made sense to them.

Beyond all of these schools and individuals to whom one can attribute a particular concept or habit, dozens of other elements evident in everyday life in China also have a strong impact on Chinese leadership. For a thorough examination, the reader is referred to the excellent article by Graham and Lam in the *Harvard Business Review*.[7] Let me summarize some of the elements they discuss here.

Guan Xi (关系). This is one of the first Chinese phrases that a Western business person learns in China. It can literally be translated as "relationships," but it implies much more. A person with good *guan* *xi* is someone who has long-term relationships (preferably over generations). Also, these relationships are based on reciprocity. As we say in English: "You scratch my back, and I will scratch yours." But Chinese people keep mental notes on their reciprocity. There is a very strong expectation that people with *guan xi* will give and receive favors over a very long time.

When I first learned about this concept in China, I thought it was no big deal. Actually, it sounded just like having a good network in the West. But over time, I learned it was much stronger than a network. A network simply implies social connections. *Guan xi* is not simple in any way. It is a proven network with an understanding of reciprocity. People in China will do much more in the spirit of *guan xi* than what someone in your social network in the West might do. For example, people use their *guan xi* to get special treatment and preferred terms in business, to bend the rules and eliminate red tape, and to get things done faster or for a lower price. In exchange, both parties might be willing to hire "underqualified" relatives or associates, pay special "commissions," offer special gifts at Chinese New Year, and carry out other practices that some in the West might consider corrupt. In China, most of this is considered good business practice under the auspices of *guan xi*.

A common misconception about *guan xi*, however, is that if you have enough of it, you will succeed in China. We should be very clear that *guan xi* alone is no substitute for performance. In fact, some commentators are predicting that the influence of *guan xi* will dwindle in China.

Zhong Jian Ren (**中间人**). This term refers to a business colleague or associate with whom you have worked for a long time and in whom you have very strong trust. This person can be used to work out with others details that might be controversial or even negative. Rather than saying "no" directly to someone, you could use your *zhong jian ren*.[8]

This concept is also related to the idea of being less direct than Westerners in one's contact with others. Westerners also use attorneys and other "stand-ins" to handle certain very detailed or perhaps contentious matters, but when it comes to negotiations, they usually prefer to handle things directly. Chinese leaders prefer to leave these sensitive matters to others and only get involved at the "hand-shaking" phase.

For Westerners, the *zhong jian ren* can also help in understanding non-verbal communications among Chinese. For example, silence in Chinese may mean there is resistance. It is also difficult for even the most fluent Chinese-speaking Westerner to understand the real meaning behind the words. In these cases, the *zhong jian ren* is a very valuable addition to the Western leader's team.

Zheng Ti Guan Nian (**整体观念**).   This term is best translated to represent what Westerners call "holistic thinking." Westerners are trained in a kind of scientific thinking that is very linear. When dealing with a problem, they tend to break it down into parts and consider the matter with deductive reasoning. Chinese are raised to think much more holistically. They consider all parts of a matter at once and have no problem reviewing matters over and over again. Westerners tend to be more orderly in their thinking and are often frustrated by this type of process.

If we can accept that our leaders will most comfortably represent the values they were raised with, we can see how leaders in China might see their roles differently from leaders in the West. Likewise, employees will expect their leaders to represent certain values and may be uncomfortable with any variance from these.

In the next chapter, we will examine some of the unique traits required for leading in China. These are indeed different from those that are most often quoted in Western leadership books.

Notes

1   Wing-Tsit Chan, *A Sourcebook in Chinese Philosophy* (Princeton, NJ: Princeton University Press, 1969).

2   Patricia Buckley Ebrey, *China* (London: Cambridge University Press, 1996).

3   Robert E. Buswell, Jr. (ed.), *Chinese Buddhist Apocrypha* (Honolulu, HI: University of Hawaii Press, 1990).

4   Arthur F. Wright, *Studies in Chinese Buddhism* R. Somers (ed.) (New Haven, CT: Yale University Press, 1990).

5   Jasper Becker, *The Chinese* (New York: The Free Press, 2000).

6   Sun Zi, *The Art of War* (Internet; English translation found on various public websites).

7   John L. Graham and N. Mark Lam, "The Chinese Negotiation," *Harvard Business Review*, Vol. 81, No. 10, October 2003, pp. 82–91.

8   *Ibid.*, p. 86.

Chapter Five Executive Summary

Philosophical and Cultural Foundations of Chinese Leadership

- We cannot generalize too much about Chinese culture, as it is a huge country with different cultural underpinnings in all of its provinces and among the various age groups.

- Chinese culture is deeply founded in Confucianism, Daoism, and Buddhism. They were all suppressed during the Cultural Revolution, but none was eradicated. Today, they again have special significance in China. Each of these philosophies has numerous off-shoots, so it is sometimes necessary to qualify your reference to these schools by specifying the branch to which you are referring.

- Confucianism teaches virtue, order, and harmony. There are countless proverbs attributed to Confucius that Chinese people often quote and try to aspire to. The best-known leaders in China are said to be modeled after the Confucian approach.

- Daoism (道, the Way) refers to the natural flow of things in the world. It is not composed of rules, as is Confucianism, but rather describes a path that one should follow. The well-known concepts of *yin* (阴) and *yang* (阳) are derived from Daoism.

- Buddhism teaches reflection and self-awareness. Many important leadership concepts, such as *wu* (悟, very deep insight), are founded in Buddhism.

- In addition to these schools of thought (or religions, as regarded by some people), there are individuals who have had a strong influence on modern Chinese thinking. These include Sun Zi, Sun Yat Sen, Mao Zedong, and Deng Xiaoping.

- There are also many Chinese concepts, not attributed to any particular school of thought or individual, that have been important in China for centuries and continue to be very important in everyday life, and certainly in business leadership. These include long-term reciprocal relationships (关系, *guan xi*), the use of trusted middle men (中间人, *zhong jian ren*), and holistic thinking (整体观念, *zheng ti guan nian*).

Chapter 6

UNIQUE LEADERSHIP TRAITS IN CHINA

Many who study the differences between Chinese and Western leadership point out that Western leadership typically depends on a given relationship between the leader and the followers. But this is entirely based on a cultural assumption that such a relationship must exist. In some cultures, such as China, there is no assumption that there needs to be a relationship between the leader and his or her employees. In China, the leader is there and so are the employees. The idea that there should be some kind of personal relationship between these two entities is entirely Western. While the power-distance between the leader and the followers in China is becoming smaller, it is still the foundation for the differences in leadership traits required of Chinese and Western leaders.

If we ask Westerners what traits they want in a leader, they tend to describe features that assume there is a relationship between them and the leader. There is no need to repeat here a long list of common Western leadership traits, as these can be found in hundreds of books and articles. However, typically, these lists would include traits such as honesty, the ability to build trust, empathy, emotional intelligence, courage, and encouragement of teamwork and ethical work practices. But when we ask Chinese what they look for in a leader, the answer is quite different. While Chinese people like to see those same kinds of things in a leader that Westerners seek, their focus is very different. The traits suggested are not so much about how the leader relates to others, but rather are descriptive of the leader as an entity in and of himself.

The traits that leaders in China mention most often are: *wu* (悟), *zhong yong* (中庸), patriotism, integrating Western best practices with Chinese wisdom, holistic thinking, and, interestingly, indirectness. Let us take a look at each of these from the perspectives of the Chinese leaders who were interviewed.

Wu (悟)

One leadership trait that one rarely hears about from Westerners is what the Chinese refer to as *wu* (悟). Many of the Chinese leaders we interviewed referred to it.

Gao Yong of Career International described *wu* as meaning "very deep insight." Many Chinese believe that this is a special trait in Chinese leaders that is probably not able to be developed by Westerners. It comes from a holistic worldview that requires the use of all five senses in understanding a situation. (The Chinese character for *wu* consists of two parts: on the left is the character for "heart," while on the right side are the five senses on top of the character for "mouth." Literally, this could be interpreted as "using your mouth to ask questions, but then using your five senses—and, ultimately, your heart—for understanding.")

Fang Yulan, in his well-read book on Chinese culture, adds to the description of *wu* by elaborating on what he calls the "five functions," rather than five senses. He describes these as follows: "The first of these is personal appearance; the second, speech; the third, vision; the fourth, hearing; and the fifth, thought. ... (For the person with a high level of wu (悟) personal appearance will be decorous; speech should be orderly; vision should be clear; hearing, distinct; and thought profound."[1]

> *"One of the key traits for a Chinese leader is 'wu' (悟). It is difficult to translate this into English since it is a very Eastern concept. It implies an extremely deep understanding. It cannot really be taught. It comes from being brought up Chinese and having exposure to Chinese wisdom. The Japanese call this 'satori,' which means a kind of enlightenment. But in a Chinese business sense, it means that you use all of your senses to understand something. It is not a matter of degree of understanding, but rather the quality of understanding. I do not think Westerners can have this competency because Westerners tend to think in a linear way. This is not linear thinking. It is holistic thinking and is a typical way for a Chinese leader to think about something."*
>
> **Gao Yong**, *President, Career International, Inc., Beijing, China.*

I do not agree with Gao Yong that Westerners cannot have this ability. But I do agree that Westerners typically do not think this way. Western leaders in China should be aware that there is an expectation by their Chinese counterparts and employees that they do not use *wu*. If one is seen as making rash judgments and decisions without giving them much thought, as Western leaders often do, Chinese employees will see this negatively.

Li Jianbo of Cisco Systems (China) thinks of *wu* as "very deep thinking."

> *"The Chinese leader uses his 'wu' (悟) to think something through to the core. Chinese believe that to make a decision, you really need to see through the outside into the core. You can only do this with 'wu.'"*
>
> **Li Jianbo**, *Vice President, Human Resources, Cisco Systems (China), Beijing, China.*

Janet Zhong of Alcoa has more to add about *wu*.

> *"Westerners can learn from the usage of 'wu' (悟). Every culture's leaders need deep insight, but Chinese seem to have more of it. Western leaders can easily fall back on their processes and systems. But in China, these are not so clearly defined, so we must think very deeply*
>
> *(continued)*

(continued)

about our issues. We don't have systems to work everything out. We also need to take into account Chinese history, which tells many stories of people being killed for saying the wrong things. I don't mean that Chinese leaders worry about being killed if they make mistakes, but this is a very punishing culture and leaders are very careful before they make decisions. This is where they use 'wu.'"

Janet Zhong, *Vice President, Human Resources, Asia Pacific, Alcoa (China) Investment Company, Ltd., Beijing, China.*

Zhong Yong (中庸)

Fung Yulan also introduces the idea of suddenness to the meaning of *wu*. "Ancient masters would use the metaphor of 'the bottom of a tub falling out.' When this happens, all its contents are suddenly gone. In the same way, when one uses *wu* properly, all of his problems are suddenly solved."[2]

Guo Xin of Mercer believes that another core Chinese leadership trait is *zhong yong* (中庸), the Confucian principle of avoiding extremes. This means that a leader with this ability will often move to the center on an issue, rather than decide for or against it.

"Chinese leaders follow the Confucian principle of 'zhong yong' (中庸). Literally, this means to "be in the middle." But to the Chinese leader, it means not to go to extremes. This is very different from the Western leader, who is taught to take a strong position. It can also imply having a balanced approach. Chinese leaders are quiet. They do not try to be individually recognized like the Western leader. A really good leader might not even want to be noticed.

A good example of what the Chinese leader would avoid is what happened to General Douglas MacArthur after WWII. Once he became famous and bigger than President Truman, the president sacked him. The Chinese leader will always avoid this kind of limelight and, thus, this kind of danger."

Guo Xin, *Managing Director, Greater China, Mercer Consulting, Beijing, China.*

Taking a low profile and moving to the center on an issue is definitely not what Westerners expect in their leaders. When Westerners take a firm position on an issue, especially when others feel that all sides were not fully considered, the Chinese may see the Western leader as shallow in his or her thinking. This will not garner the respect that the leader seeks.

This is what Li Jianbo of Cisco Systems says about *zhong yong*.

"The Western leadership style, at first glance, has many similarities with the Chinese. But there are fundamental differences that are subtle but very important. For example, we follow 'zhong yong.' This Confucian principle is a guide for Chinese people when they work together. Never go to extremes. If you push too hard, you get a rebound. You push, but not too hard. You lead and you push. You lead and you push. You don't push water to you. You build a canal. Water will flow to you when the canal is ready. Chinese leaders will make lots of preparation before making a move. It might involve taking two steps forward and then one step backward.

    On the other hand, Westerners are drivers. They drive people, drive goals, and drive change. This is often viewed by the Chinese as being too aggressive. We see many Western leaders violating the principle of 'zhong yong.'"

Li Jianbo, *Vice President of Human Resources, Cisco Systems (China), Beijing, China.*

I have had my own example of *zhong yong* as both a university professor in Beijing and a lecturer. In both cases, I gave the students a brief review of the Theory X and Theory Y management styles put forward by Douglas McGregor.[3] Briefly, Theory X represents a style of management that assumes workers will not work without being forced to, either by incentive or by fear. It assumes that workers are not capable of doing work without the strict reinforcement of a strong boss. Theory Y, on the other hand, assumes that workers want to do well. They just need guidance and will then do a good job.

In the West, when one describes these two extremes and then asks managers which style they believe they should follow, nearly all will lean toward Theory Y. In China, however, whenever I ask this question of my audiencess, they all indicated that they will aim toward the middle. This is *zhong yong*.

Patriotism

Victor Lang, President of MMD Asia Pacific Ltd., believes that an important difference between Western and Chinese leaders is that the Chinese leader, in addition to seeking profits like the Western leader, has a broader mission that is rooted in Chinese patriotism and a strong desire to make China a superior business power in the world.

> *"The main difference between Chinese and Western leaders is that we Chinese have much more of a social mission than Westerners. Western leaders are primarily focused on satisfying shareholders. Of course, we worry about money, too. But we have a bigger mission. We are very patriotic and try very hard to make our companies successful so that China is successful. In that regard, Chinese leaders will do anything to make our companies successful. We sometimes envy the Western leader who can focus on work–life balance. The Chinese leader knows that there is nothing more important than the company and will nearly always sacrifice family matters for company matters. I have worked for my company for 10 years and have never taken a vacation or a personal holiday. My cell phone is open for customers 24 hours a day and seven days a week."*
>
> **Victor Lang**, President, MMD Asia Pacific Ltd., Beijing, China.

One would be hard pressed in the West to find patriotism on a list of leadership traits. But in China, it is almost always found. Westerners who have lived in China for a while will notice this in both subtle and not-so-subtle ways. Leadership speeches in China often make reference to the impact the company is making on the growth of China. When, in 2007, there were many recalls of Chinese products in the West, this was seen in China as just as much a reflection on the country as on the company concerned. Many of the offending company leaders were severely and publicly punished, not so much for the business violation as for the damage they did to China's reputation on the world stage.

Integrating Best Western Practices with Chinese Wisdom

The Vice President of the TCL Institute of Leadership, Xu Fang, says that some of the specific traits TCL looks for in a leader are similar to those one might seek in the West: truthfulness, innovativeness, and insightfulness. But they also seek humility in their leaders, not a commonly found word on lists of Western leadership traits. Xu also mentions the importance of understanding Chinese culture and her assessment that Western leaders need this in order to be successful in China.

> *"A Western leader can do well in China if they are sensitive to Chinese culture. In fact, a leader who wants to teach Western practices in China can be a better teacher if they understand Chinese culture first. To be a better teacher of Western practices, you had better be a good student of Chinese culture."*
>
> **Xu Fang**, *Vice President, TCL Institute of Leadership Development, TCL Corporation, Huizhou, China.*

Victor Lang of MMD Asia echoes this point.

> *"A leader in China must understand Chinese values. If you don't, you will not be accepted by employees. But you must also understand Western practices so that your Western peers and bosses will accept you, too."*
>
> **Victor Lang**, *President, MMD Asia Pacific Ltd., Beijing, China.*

This is a key concept for any leader in China, and is the third main theme of this book. If a leader in China cannot integrate best Western practices with Chinese thinking, then he or she will inevitably fail. This is not only important for cultural reasons, as noted earlier; but it also has a more subtle, and perhaps more important, value. Having things done in a Chinese way is a major source of pride in China. The Western leader must be aware of this in order to succeed in China. Any leader, Chinese or Western, who conveys a sense of superiority because of all that they have learned from best Western practices will fail in China.

Holistic Thinking

Several leaders who were interviewed for this book felt that Chinese leaders were more holistic in their thinking than Westerners. While there are some Westerners who sometimes think this way too, for the most part, Westerners think in a linear way. Take a look at the anecdote below.

> *"Westerners tend to divide up issues into small pieces—people, processes, and systems. Chinese leaders tend to see issues much more holistically. We don't see these parts outside of the whole. When we try to solve a problem, we look at the entire issue at once. This could mean going back over things again and again. I know this approach sometimes frustrates Westerners, who prefer to deal with issues more systematically.*
>
> *A good example to describe this difference is found in medicine. A Western doctor looks at the virus and tries to find a cure for it. The Chinese doctor looks at the whole person and tries to figure out why the body had this problem."*
>
> **Li Jianbo**, *Vice President of Human Resources, Cisco Systems (China), Beijing, China.*

This trait resembles *wu* (悟), but it is actually quite different. *Wu* focuses on depth of thinking and the use of all of the senses. Holistic thinking is about breadth of thinking and the integration of all parts of an issue. Michael Bond, a noted expert on Chinese culture, believes holistic thinking in China is derived from the pictorial alphabet. "Chinese children learn to memorize thousands of pictorial characters ... because Chinese words are pictures rather than sequences of letters." As such, Bond suggests, "Chinese children are better at seeing the big picture."[4]

The downside of holistic thinking is that someone who does this exclusively may lose sight of the importance of detail by focusing just on the bigger picture. Again, this is often a cause of frustration for Westerners, who tend to be very detail oriented.

Indirectness

Chinese leaders need to know how to be direct with their subordinates. When describing the company's mission, people need to know precisely where the company intends to go. In times of crisis, the leader needs to give very direct and accurate information so that employees can best understand the new situation. So, having the trait of indirectness does not mean a leader is never direct. It just means that sometimes it is a more constructive style in China to be indirect rather than direct. This is very different from the practice in the West, where leaders are encouraged to be direct in nearly all situations.

Gao Yong of Career International gives an example of indirectness in leadership.

> *"There is an ancient Chinese king who will soon retire. He has a son who he wants to replace him as king. The king is greatly loved by his subjects. He hopes the same for his son. The king has many loyal generals. One day, he calls in his most trusted general and tells him he is being re-assigned to a very remote province. The general is very disappointed, but he follows the wishes of his king. Is this a demotion? Did he do something to upset the king to warrant the transfer? No one knows.*
>
> *In a year, the son becomes king. One year later, the son recalls the general to the capital. The general is happy and is now very grateful and loyal to the son. If the first king did not banish the general, the son could not complete this kind act. The first king never explained his motive. He just made a decision. But through his foresight, he knew that this chain of events would seal the loyalty of this great general to the new king, his son.*
>
> *Western leaders would not do it this way. Rather, they would be very direct and open about their actions. A Chinese leader may follow this indirect approach, never having to explain why they did what they did."*
>
> **Gao Yong**, President, Career International, Beijing, China.

This story is typical of the kind of indirect thinking and actions that are often seen in China. At first, no one knows the reason for the action except, perhaps, the leader who takes the action. In China, there is no need to explain this action. In fact, too much explanation defeats the purpose.

Indirectness implies thoughtfulness. It is also a safe course, as it is easier to renege on an indirect action than a more clearly defined, direct one.

It is also considered a trait of subordinates to "guess" what the leader is thinking. I have a Chinese friend who works for a large international accounting firm in Beijing. When working for a former Chinese boss, she often had to try and guess what her boss really wanted, because he would never tell her directly. She said it was like a game among her colleagues. The best of them were able to figure out what the most desirable course of action was.

Why is this? Why not just tell people directly what you want them to do?

Shi Lan of Towers Perrin in Beijing believes this is related to the leader's concern with making a public mistake. While private firms rarely espouse this behavior, it is still very common among SOEs.

> *"In state-owned enterprises, the leader does not want to make a public mistake. Their goal is often not to grow the enterprise, but rather to be promoted to a higher level. We have a saying, 'tao guang yang hui' (韬光养晦). This means that you hide your capabilities. You just don't let others know what you know. This practice is not at all encouraged in multinational firms, but the Chinese practice has been infused into managers and leaders for a long time. This is also why we Chinese are often accused of not being innovative or risk-taking. The more you show of yourself publicly, the more likely you can be accused of making a mistake."*
>
> **Shi Lan**, *Senior Consultant for Leadership, Towers Perrin, Beijing, China.*

Any list of leadership traits is incomplete, as the real number is infinite. But those described in this chapter were the ones most often quoted by Chinese leaders and Chinese leadership experts who were interviewed for this book. But there are others that some leaders mentioned as being significant for their own success as leaders in China. While they were not brought up by others and therefore were not given specific focus in this chapter, I have personally observed other leaders demonstrate these additional competencies in my own work. Therefore, I want to at least mention them here because I believe they are useful and, with a larger sample than this book used, they may have been statistically significant.

Customer Sacrifice.   It was noted earlier that Victor Lang of MMD Asia leaves his cell phone on 24 hours a day, seven days a week.

> *"My cell phone is always on. Western leaders won't do this. They are more interested in having some work–life balance. But Chinese customers demand this. Most Chinese leaders will put off a planned vacation for customer reasons. I have been with MMD for 10 years and have never taken one day off. I am always open to my customers' needs."*
>
> **Victor Lang**, *President, MMD Asia Pacific Ltd., Beijing, China.*

In my experience, this is an extreme example of customer sacrifice. But it is not as farfetched as many Westerners might imagine. I have had examples at both Watson Wyatt and Hewitt where clients required consultants to be available at all hours of the day and night and on weekends. One consultant was scheduled to attend a relative's wedding on a Saturday. The client, a well-known company in China, insisted that she forego the wedding in order to attend a last-minute strategy meeting that they had called. Another client would call me and others at the firm after 10:00 p.m. to discuss what I considered to be mundane matters. A third client insisted that a consultant who was scheduled to sit for her Ph.D. exam on a particular Saturday not take the exam so that she could participate in the client's board meeting that had been scheduled long after her exam was scheduled. In all of these cases, I objected and took a stand with the clients, saying these requests were inappropriate and that we should make other arrangements.

I am still not sure if I was right or wrong in these cases, but I know that the clients were not pleased, even though we figured out suitable alternatives to their requests. Victor Lang believes that good leaders in China need to be extremely flexible and meet these customer demands.

Humanistic. Gao Yong of Career International thinks that he pays more attention to employees than most Western managers would, and even more so than many other Chinese managers.

> *"CEOs and other leaders need to worry about their employees' housing needs, children's schooling, parents' health, and other personal matters. Even though I am limited in what I can do, I must at least show my willingness to help.*
>
> *By the way, I must ask first. The employee would rarely bring up such a problem. It is the leader's job to introduce the topic."*
>
> **Gao Yong**, *President, Career International, Inc., Beijing, China.*

At first, this trait may seem at odds with the earlier discussion of power-distance. One might ask, "If Chinese culture advocates a high power-distance between the leader and those being led, why would a leader care to be humanistic?" We should not confuse this natural tendency to be distant with the very different issue of being humanistic. A leader can show care and concern for his or her employees, as described above by Gao Yong, even though the dominant culture may dictate that, in daily operations, the leader remains distant from the workers. In fact, when the leader does demonstrate humanism within a high power-distance culture, the gestures are often considered much more special than they might be in a low power-distance culture where such displays would be expected. An example of this was when Chinese Premier Wen Jiabao went quickly to the site of the Sichuan earthquake in 2008 and called out to people still buried in the rubble: "This is Uncle Wen. I will help you. Hold on a little longer." Likewise, when the Qinghai earthquake struck in 2010, President Hu Jintao went to the site and spoke with survivors, referring to himself as "Grandpa Hu" and assuring them that everything would soon be fine. He would see to it, he said, that everyone received proper care, and that the town would be rebuilt.

Long-Term View. Li Jianbo of Cisco Systems believes that a successful leader in China needs to have a long-term view of the company and should inspire a long-term relationship with employees.

> *"When a leader begins a relationship with an employee, both parties need to see this as the beginning of a long-term relationship. Sometimes leaders cannot see past the need to generate profits in the short term. But if we do not also look beyond the horizon, employees will soon tire of the endless struggle for short-term profits and become dissatisfied with the firm and with the boss."*
>
> **Li Jianbo**, Vice President, Human Resources, Cisco Systems (China), Beijing, China.

This concept is also related to relationships. It is difficult to build up *guan xi* with just short-term thinking. As John Graham and Mark Lam point out, in the West, "sizing up takes minutes. In China, this may last days, weeks, even months."[5]

In the next chapter, we will examine one very special leadership trait that is highly admired by Chinese employees: leading from the heart. Before we move on to the chapters that look more closely at various leadership issues in China, let us take a look at what underlies all of this—human resource trends in China.

Notes

1   Yulan Fung, *A Short History of Chinese Philosophy* (New York: The Free Press, 1948), p. 132.
2   *Ibid.*, p. 262.
3   Douglas McGregor, *The Human Side of Intervention* (New York: McGraw-Hill, 1960).
4   John L. Graham and N. Mark Lam, "The Chinese Negotiation," *Harvard Business Review*, Vol. 81, No. 10, October 2003, pp. 82–91.
5   *Ibid.*, p. 85.
6   *Ibid.*, p. 87.

Chapter Six Executive Summary

Unique Leadership Traits in China

- Western leadership traits are, for the most part, dependent on an intended relationship between the leader and his or her followers. These might include traits such as honesty, the ability to build trust, empathy, emotional intelligence, courage, and the encouragement of teamwork and ethical work practices.

- Chinese employees will look for these same Western competencies in a leader, but they also distinguish their own leaders based on other traits that are unique to China. These include: *wu* (悟, very deep insight), *zhong yong* (中庸, not going to extremes), patriotism, integrating Western best practices with Chinese wisdom, and indirectness.

- *Wu* is based on Buddhism and refers to the leader's ability to understand an issue from its core. The Chinese character for *wu* (悟) includes pictures of the five senses, implying that these are all required for this type of understanding. The Japanese refer to this concept as *satori,* which is a form of enlightenment. While the Chinese use *wu* more in a business sense than a mystical sense, it nevertheless implies this very deep understanding.

- *Zhong yong* (中庸) is a Confucian concept whose literal meaning is "to be in the middle." But the actual meaning for leaders is "to not go to extremes." Chinese leaders often seek consensus from their top managers. This is a safer approach than taking an extreme position. The concept is also related to the Daoist ideas of balance and harmony.

- Chinese leaders are expected to be patriotic. While their bosses require allegiance to the firm, Chinese society also expects allegiance to the country.

- Leaders in China are expected to express themselves much less directly than those in the West. Indirectness implies thoughtfulness and also allows room for renegotiation after the fact. A more direct approach may be seen as too final and inflexible.

- Three other unique Chinese leadership traits were mentioned by just one interviewee each. As such, they were not listed among those that received multiple mentions. However, they are still worth noting and describing briefly. These were customer sacrifice, striving to be humanistic, and holding a long-term view.

Chapter 7

LEADING FROM THE HEART

In the previous chapter, we looked at the unique traits of Chinese leaders and saw that there are specific differences between Chinese and Western leaders. However, there is one theme that underscores all of these traits and is central to successful business leadership in China: leading from the heart.

Many other writers have addressed this theme, although not specifically in regard to China. In *The Leadership Challenge*, perhaps the most widely read leadership book in the world, James Kouzes and Barry Posner identify "encouraging the heart" as one of the five practices of an exemplary leader.[1] The Center for Creative Leadership (CCL) identifies "caring" as one of the five most influential characteristics of an effective leader. According to CCL, this means that the leader shows a sincere interest in and genuine concern for others.[2] Jack Kahl titled his 2004 book *Leading from the Heart: Choosing to Be a Servant Leader*.[3] His primary theme is that being a servant leader involves caring deeply for the people you are leading. That is certainly part of it. Daniel Goleman, in *Emotional Intelligence*,[4] made the case that non-cognitive skills can be as important as IQ for workforce success. In a later work, *Primal Leadership*,[5] co-authored with Richard Boyatizis and Annie McKee,

Goleman demonstrates how these skills also relate positively to leadership success. Even the famed Duke University basketball coach, Mike Krzyewski, titled his book *Leading from the Heart: Coach K's Successful Strategies for Basketball, Business, and Life.*[6]

In an e-zine article, executive coach Jayne Warrilow describes leading from the heart this way: "Leading from the heart requires a willingness to look within, and to have developed a greater level of self-awareness than most. It requires that leaders know themselves and how emotions have a fundamental impact on our behavior and decision-making and ultimately on our people. It requires developing a leadership presence, so that we can be there for our people, recognizing others' emotions and managing relationships successfully."[7]

So, how does this all relate to leading in China? Angie Wei, a senior leadership consultant at Hewitt Associates, talks about this when describing what makes leaders admired in China.

> *"We like our leaders here to demonstrate a caring approach. Westerners show caring through processes such as listening and empowering. But in China, we want that caring to be very genuine; not just something that a leader has learned to do."*
>
> **Angie Wei**, *Senior Consultant, Hewitt Associates, Beijing, China.*

This quote reminds me of a story I heard as a young man about the famous musical conductor, Leonard Bernstein. An interviewer asked him what he felt was the secret to his success. His answer was that he "loved" his audience. The Chinese leader who leads from the heart displays this same type of deep caring for his or her employees' success and well-being.

> *"Some leaders use their brains to lead. I try very hard to use my heart."*
>
> **Kelly Wang**, *Founder and Director, GW Technologies Co. Ltd., Beijing, China.*

One Chinese business leader who is highly admired is Dr. Liu Jiren. Dr. Liu is the Founder, Chairman, and CEO of Neusoft

Corporation, China's leading software development and IT services firm. Liu has received many awards in China for leadership. In 2009, he was named as one of the top 10 "Economic Persons of the Year" in China by China Central Television (CCTV), China's national TV station. In an interview with David Michael of The Boston Consulting Group in 2010, Liu had the following to say about his leadership style. "You need to be open-minded, listen to all sides, be sensitive to the environment, and then make decisions. ... If you trust people and give them an opportunity to show their value, people will be passionate about their work. Money is important to employees, but it is not as important as some people think."[8]

Some people in China say that employees stay at Neusoft primarily because of their loyalty to and admiration for Liu Jiren. He typifies what was referred to in an earlier chapter as a *junzi* (君子, gentleman).

Another highly admired Chinese leader is Ren Jianxin, President of the China National Chemical Corporation, more commonly referred to as Chem China. Like Liu Jiren, Ren Jianxin is a recipient of numerous leadership awards, including the CCTV "Economic Persons of the Year" in 2007 and the Federation of Chinese Entrepreneurs' "Entrepreneur of the Year" in 2006. Ren is also considered to lead from the heart. In an article in the *McKinsey Quarterly*, Ren described one of the key responsibilities of his office as being to create jobs for society. "As an entrepreneur, I have to try as hard as I can to create jobs for the unfortunate. Since the chemical industry was laying off so many people in China, I created a service business, Malan Noodle, which has become the number one fast-food chain in China. It has taken on more than 10,000 workers who used to be employees of former chemical companies that were streamlined through acquisition."[9]

A third Chinese leader who is often admired for his "leading from the heart" approach is Wang Shi, Founder and Chairman of the largest real estate company in China, Vanke. According to a piece published in the *Architectural Record*, "Wang does not fit the stereotype of the wheeling-and-dealing Chinese property developer. ... [He] sprinkles his conversation with references to American psychologist Abraham Maslow's hierarchy of needs."[10] The implication is that this hierarchy applies to employees in the firm who have different needs at different stages of their lives. Wang believes the corporation must address these different needs.

These examples of admired leaders are not intended to imply that all leaders in China lead from the heart. Actually, the opposite is true. Most leaders in China achieved their positions through struggle and/or opportunity. Think of all of the leaders in the Yangtze and Pearl River deltas who built their firms from scratch. Many of them started out in business as street peddlers. The insatiable need from abroad for cheap Chinese-made products quickly elevated these business founders to positions of prominence. But most of these leaders rely on their instincts, not their hearts, for guidance on how to lead. Their primary motivation is profit; only as a secondary matter do they consider the well-being of their employees.

> *"Many Chinese leaders got to their positions through opportunity and good luck. Many are not well educated. They are often demanding and aggressive. These leaders are followed because they are the bosses, but they are not admired. I do not expect to see this type of leader in the future in China. This kind of money-focused leadership cannot be sustained as employees become more interested in what really makes them fulfilled. If the leader does not respect them, they will not respect the leader."*
>
> **Angie Wei**, *Senior Consultant, Hewitt Associates, Beijing, China.*

Leadership Styles in China

Among the many features of leadership that a leader must be concerned with is their leadership *style*. In business leadership, "style" refers to the recurring patterns of one's behavior. While every leader will have a unique style, the dominant styles of leaders in a company will help to shape the organization's culture. In China, there are as many different leadership styles as there are leaders, but there appear to be some patterns that are generally representative of the Chinese style of leadership.

Human Synergistics, an Australia-headquartered organization development company, has identified 12 styles that research has shown to be directly related to leadership.[11] To measure the degree of presence of these styles, they developed a 360-degree tool aimed at capturing a leader's intended styles and then comparing those to the styles that the leader is perceived to have by those who work with him or her. The tool is called the Life Styles Inventory (LSI)™. Four of these dozen styles fall into the "constructive" category. The remaining eight are classified as "destructive," in that they are defensive in nature. While all leaders will occasionally use defensive styles of leadership, the best business performance is achieved when key leaders demonstrate the constructive styles. For a detailed description of each style identified by Human Synergistics, the reader is referred to their website.[12] While there is no published research on how these styles are specifically demonstrated in China, I have made my own observations. I have administered the LSI to over 100 executives in China over the past four years. In that sample, the styles that are most prevalent are *Approval, Avoidance, Power,* and *Competitive*. Each of these is considered by Human Synergistics as defensive styles. The first two are further labeled as "passive defensive" and the latter two as "aggressive defensive."

A leader with a high score on *Approval* will often display behavior that implies the need to be accepted by others in order to increase their feelings of self-worth. Characteristics of this style include low self-esteem, a deep concern with the opinion of others, and a strong desire to be well liked. A high *Avoidance* score means that the leader often withdraws from dealing with matters that he or she perceives as personally threatening. Characteristics may include feelings of self-doubt and avoidance of decision-making. *Power* reflects a tendency to control others. Leaders who are high on this style will come across to others as aggressive and as lacking confidence in others' abilities. Leaders who score high on the *Competitive* style may be demonstrating the need to achieve feelings of high self-worth through competing against and comparing themselves to others. These leaders are preoccupied with winning and have a strong fear of failure.[13]

These observations are not intended to suggest that all Chinese leaders will primarily demonstrate the four styles identified above. As I noted earlier, these are observations based on my own review of LSI results and not the result of scientific research by Human Synergistics or any other organization. Nevertheless, these observations have been fairly consistent and, in my view, are typical of many leaders in China. That is why those admired leaders who are known for "leading from the heart" are unique. But this is exactly the leadership style that anyone leading in China should aspire to develop.

Perceptions and Misperceptions of Leadership Style

One of the more interesting outcomes of the use of this kind of 360-degree tool is the realization by some leaders, when told the results of their LSIs, that the people they lead often perceive their behavior quite differently than how the leader intended. When a leader is presented with these findings, their response may be one of surprise or even skepticism. In one case, the LSI was administered to the CEO of a major chemical company in China. Although he thought he was being very achievement oriented, he learned that his subordinates interpreted his behavior quite differently; they saw him as being competitive, a perfectionist, and focused on his need for personal power. This discrepancy between how he thought he was perceived, and how he was actually perceived, by his subordinates caused the executive to decide to change his leadership style. We based our coaching sessions on these findings, and he developed a self-improvement plan based specifically on changing his behaviors so as to improve the way he was perceived.

The CEO of a large European manufacturing firm located in China was also initially surprised by his LSI results. He even questioned the validity of the testing instrument and the methodology. I asked him if he wished to solicit independent validation from the people who had assessed him. He decided not to ask them for their individual confidential responses; instead, he shared with them his general findings, especially those that had surprised him. The feedback he received supported the findings. After three of these sessions, he was convinced. He then set out on a clear self-improvement path that included the sincere request to his subordinates to tell him if they saw him going off track. After a year, he repeated the styles test and found a significant improvement. His constructive styles were much more in evidence than the year before, and the defensive styles less so. He did the test again the following year and his results had continued to improve.

Employee Reaction to Leadership Style Changes

Research has demonstrated that very aggressive leaders breed very passive subordinates. If a leader wants employees who work constructively and confidently to achieve results, and if he or she wishes to assist those subordinates in their growth, then the leader also needs to be seen to be constructive in his or her own approach. In my experience, there is about a one-year delay in changing the organization's leadership style after the top leader changes his or her style. But it does happen! One Chinese high-tech company experienced major positive changes in its leadership culture, but the changes did not come about organizationally until after it was clear that the top leader had modified his own leadership style and was expecting the same of his subordinates.

It makes sense in *any* country to lead from the heart. But if you do so in China, the financial rewards are substantial and your employees will hold you in much higher regard.

Notes

1 James M. Kouzes and Barry Z. Posner, *The Leadership Challenge*, 3rd edition (San Francisco: Jossey-Bass, 2002).
2 Gene Klann, "Leadership Character: Five Essential Characteristics," *Center for Creative Leadership* (podcast), www.ccl.org.
3 Jack Kahl, *Leading from the Heart: Choosing to Be a Servant Leader* (Westlake, OH: Kahl & Associates, 2004).
4 Daniel Goleman, *Emotional Intelligence* (New York: Bantam Books, 1995).
5 Daniel Goleman, *et al.*, *Primal Leadership: Realizing the Power of Emotional Intelligence* (Boston: Harvard Business School Publishing, 2002).
6 Mike Krzyewski, *et al.*, *Leading from the Heart: Coach K's Successful Strategies for Basketball, Business, and Life* (Victoria, Australia: Warner Books, 2001).

7 Jayne Warrilow, "Leading from the Heart," Ezine articles.com, April 30, 2010.

8 David Michael, "Managing Rapid Growth," Interview with Liu Jiren, Leadership.bcg.com, February 2010.

9 Tomas Koch and Oliver Ramsbottom, "A Growth Strategy for a Chinese State-Owned Enterprise," *McKinsey Quarterly*, July 2008, p. 6.

10 Frederick Balfour, "China Vanke Company," *Architectural Record*, April 2008.

11 Human Synergistics International, Life Styles Inventory™.

12 www.humansynergistics.com.

13 These descriptions come from the Human Synergistics guide. For a more detailed description with specific examples, please consult the Human Synergistics website as noted in the prior endnote.

Chapter Seven Executive Summary

Leading from the Heart

- Leading from the heart is an essential trait of admired leaders in China.

- There have been many books written on this subject around the world. In order to see the importance of applying this concept in China, however, one needs to study some of the leaders in China who are held in very high regard.

- The majority of leaders in China do not lead from the heart. They achieved their current positions by being cunning, aggressive, and opportunistic. But the more admired leaders do clearly demonstrate this characteristic. These are the ones whose styles will be sustainable.

- There are certain behavioral patterns in every leader that are unique to that individual. These may be identified through 360-degree evaluation.

- Leadership styles that are prevalent in China are: seeking approval, avoiding certain issues, demonstrating power, and acting competitively. Each of these styles is considered destructive and not conducive to leading from the heart.

- Leaders can be tested for their styles through psychometric tools that capture 360-degree information. Often, the leader's behavior is perceived differently by employees than the leader intended.

- Leaders can be coached to increase their constructive styles and decrease their destructive styles. The intention is to develop styles that demonstrate leading from the heart.

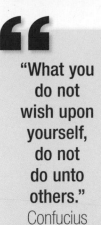

> "What you do not wish upon yourself, do not do unto others."
> Confucius

Chapter 8

HUMAN RESOURCE TRENDS IN CHINA

Not too long ago, most Western human resources departments concerned themselves primarily with hiring, rewards, titles, organization design, organization culture, training and development, measuring human resources, and succession planning. These were all considered to be the business of the HR department. Today, the focus is on the same "kinds" of things, but with a very different business emphasis. These issues are now referred to more as business matters, rather than HR programs. We use terms such as *attraction* and *retention*, *organization restructuring*, *employee engagement*, *competency development*, *return on human capital*, *leadership development*, and *flatter and more flexible structures*. In my experience in China, the most sophisticated HR departments are making the same subtle, but highly significant, changes. What we have is a change from a "human resources department" to a "business department that focuses on the use of people to gain competitive advantage in the market." In other words, the HR department is gradually transitioning from a transactional department to a strategic one.

Let us take a look at some of the specific trends taking place.

Employment Philosophy

When I first started working after college 40 years ago, I was told that if I worked hard and did a good job, I could be sure of regular growth in my salary, my title, and my responsibilities. In other words, my career advancement would be predictable. Isn't this similar to how it used to be in China? It sounds like the "iron rice bowl" (铁饭碗, *tie fan wan*).

But then things started to change. As we moved into a new world order, business became a much more international phenomenon. Financial success was no longer simply dependent on the economy of the country but was interwoven with world economics. Furthermore, employees were asked to assume much more business risk. No longer was career advancement guaranteed or predictable. Employees needed to take more responsibility for their own skills development and career progression. These changes took place over many years in the West. In China, employees have been asked to understand and implement these changes within a very short time frame. For some companies in China, this philosophy is still not well received. But it clearly is happening, and many companies here have already figured out how to be very successful in this relatively new market-based economy.

Reward Program Management

Companies in China, like in the West, have been revisiting their pay philosophies and strategies. When I first came to China in 2001, many companies would ask my consulting firm to install a pay system "just like all the others we had installed." They believed in the concept we refer to in the US as "one size fits all." But just as this idea disappeared many years ago in the West, it has gradually disappeared in China as well. Now companies here are interested in customizing their reward systems so that they can be used strategically. This means first understanding the reasons for various forms of reward plans, and identifying which results and behaviors should be rewarded. This, in turn, leads to decisions about how those results and behaviors should be rewarded—with base pay, incentives, developmental programs, and many other cash and non-cash reward vehicles. This kind of thinking, in turn, leads to a total remuneration approach with multiple pay elements, each having its own special purpose. While I do not see this approach used universally in China, it is moving in that direction as companies realize that using rewards differentially is a more cost-effective and success-based approach than simply doling out more money in the form of base salary.

Related to the matter of what and how to reward is the concept of how we manage the distribution of rewards in the firm. This concept is based on how we value individuals in our firms. Should we reward people exclusively for their productivity, or are there other matters that also deserve to be rewarded? These other matters include the attainment of new or higher levels of competencies, as well as the employees' ability to take on more responsibilities in the form of broader jobs. As companies in the West have been doing more of this, they have also been advancing employees for their improvement in competency development, not just for their ability to produce results. The types of rewards these more competent individuals receive may differ from those given to employees who are just more financially productive. In sales, for example, a successful salesman who consistently produces good sales results, but does not acquire the necessary traits to lead others, may find himself being placed on a sales track rather than a management track. This dual career track approach allows a company to reward people for what they are good at and not try to force them into positions where they are likely to fail. Some of the best salespeople are terrible managers, and some of the best sales managers are not the best salespeople. A dual career track helps a company keep its best people in jobs where they can best help the firm.

However, there is a noticeable problem in China with the dual career track. It is still very much expected in China that one will be promoted regularly and given grander titles commensurate with one's individual performance. Nearly everyone wants to be called a manager. What some companies have done successfully here is to use the title of "manager" liberally. Even if an employee is on a non-management track or does not manage others, the employee may still be given the title of "manager" in order to provide face. While this approach is typically not followed in the West because of the possibility of confusion, it can be used pretty easily in China.

All of this falls under the subject of "pay for performance." Performance does not have to mean just productivity results. It can also mean the display of key competencies that the company has identified for future corporate success. This can lead to a greater use of incentives than before. But for incentives to be successful, they must be tied to measurable performance. People should be told in advance of what is required to receive an incentive payment, and they should not receive such an incentive if the requirements are not met. This is a best Western practice that has met with some resistance in China, since people here often expect to get every amount of cash that is possible for them to receive. While the idea of being paid only for achieving a specific target is not easily received by Chinese employees, it has definitely caught on at many companies and will soon become as routine as it now is in the West.

Also within the area of reward program management is the focus on external competitiveness, rather than internal equity. Now that there is an adequate amount of compensation data available in China, this concept is increasingly being followed.

Executive Compensation

Recently, Chinese firms have begun following the Western practice of paying executives differently from other employees. This is not only in order to be competitive with world markets, but also because of the recognition that executives typically have a longer-term impact on a company than other employees. As such, reward programs for executives are increasingly acknowleding this greater contribution and paying them accordingly. Along with this is the stronger focus on incentives and "at-risk" pay. We are also seeing more and more Chinese firms focusing on a kind of flex plan where executives are able to choose among several options offered. This allows companies to give executives what they most need, while limiting company costs. We are seeing this trend catching on more in the area of benefits than cash compensation, but it is a growing trend.

Stock options have also become increasingly popular in China. With the help of attorneys and/or executive compensation experts, local firms have figured out ways to do this without violating Chinese laws on the buying of shares in non-Chinese firms. This is often done through a form of phantom stock and uses a third party to administer the programs in a cashless way.

A later chapter discusses the subject of reward program management in detail and makes suggestions about which elements of reward programs work best in China.

Performance Management

Performance management programs have become increasingly sophisticated over the past few years. Most notably, we are now seeing "performance" broadly defined to include competencies as well as results. Many Chinese firms include competency attainment in their performance management programs. The best programs are also aligned with corporate measures as a pre-condition. We are also seeing in China more use of comprehensive performance measures, such as the balanced scorecard, where executives and their teams are measured by more than just financial measures. These measures could include product quality, talent development or retention, and individual development areas.

In the past, one's immediate supervisor was typically the sole person measuring one's performance. Now it is quite common to receive feedback from multiple sources, including peers and subordinates. Also, individuals are now sometimes measured by group or team performance, not just their own performance.

Leadership Development

Leadership development is a worldwide trend, but it is particularly necessary in China. There is only a relatively small number of experienced people in China who have led others in regional or international business environments. As such, Chinese firms are following the lead of their Western counterparts and aggressively identifying and developing future leaders. This development occurs in the form of executive coaching, rotational and other developmental assignments, special compensation programs, developmental workshops, action learning projects, and training.

Human Resources Department

Companies around the world are aware of the need to change the human resources function from a purely transactional one to a strategic one. China is no different. When I first arrived in China, it was rare that the HR department had a seat at the executive table. HR managers and directors were often just "front men" for the senior executives who made all the corporate decisions. Oftentimes, Communist Party officials appointed them to their jobs as a reward for prior service in the military or the government. Now, we see very professional HR leaders in Chinese firms. These people are asked to lead all matters related to the use of people for competitive advantage. I saw the transition in the focus from transaction to strategy occur in the US over an approximate 20-year period. In China, it has happened in just five years. Also, HR teams are growing rapidly in terms of experience. When I first arrived in China, it was uncommon to find a team of HR experts in the department. Typically, the employees were trained only in transaction management and administration. That is no longer the case, as universities are cranking out human resources-trained graduates at a very rapid rate and they are securing jobs in the best companies in China.

As you can see, the HR trends in China are very similar to those elsewhere in the world, and especially in the US. It should come as no surprise then that, as business becomes more of an international phenomenon rather than a single-country one, the practices that are used successfully in one country are soon adopted by other countries as well.

Making it Work in China

We have looked closely at the differences in leadership cultures between China and the West, and we have examined the unique traits that are found among China's business leaders. We have also compared Chinese HR trends with those seen in the West. But the big question remains: How do we lead in China? How can we integrate the best of the West and the best of China so that we can be more effective business leaders in China?

The second part of this book offers several chapters that focus specifically on some of the most notable cultural clashes between China and the West and their impact on leadership. Their purpose is to provide real-life examples of how to succeed when faced with these dilemmas. We will begin with the often-found conflict between truth and courtesy.

Chapter Eight Executive Summary

Human Resource Trends in China

- Globally, human resources management has transformed from a transactional function to a strategic one. While this was not the case just a few years ago in China, in most multinational firms and the larger, more sophisticated Chinese domestic firms, the climate has now changed dramatically. HR executives in these firms are slowly but surely finding their place at the leadership table.

- Not too long ago in China, the government granted a person a job, and the employee could be reasonably certain of keeping it no matter how well he or she performed. As China has moved from a planned to a market economy, the situation has changed dramatically. While there are still remnants of the old philosophy, especially in domestic firms, the employment philosophy today is now much more like that found in the West.

- Reward programs in China are becoming more strategic and have borrowed greatly from those found in the West. While there continue to be needs and nuances that are specific to China, rewards are now being used much more strategically than in the days when remuneration was simply a money distribution system and not a tool to make the firm more competitive in the market for talent. "Paying for performance" is now a commonly used term in China. Only 10 years ago, it was an alien concept. Some firms are now recognizing the special contribution that executives make and are paying them accordingly. In a later chapter, we will take a closer look at reward program management in China.

- Companies in China now have fairly sophisticated methods of managing performance, similar to those found in the West. It is not uncommon to find companies including competency attainment, as well as productivity results measurement, in their plans. Just as in the West, Chinese firms are beginning to use multi-rater assessment rather than just supervisor review.

- As noted in the first chapter, finding and retaining leaders is among the toughest HR challenges in China. As such, there is a growing

(continued)

(continued)

trend toward helping leaders in the firm to develop their skills quickly. In fact, because of the enormous need in China, one could argue that the leadership development trend is more apparent in China than elsewhere in the world.

- The HR department in China has become increasingly important over the past few years. In the past, HR leadership jobs were often held by former Communist Party cadres who were placed in human resources as a reward for their past performances in the Party. They were not necessarily HR experts. Today, that is not the case. Most multinational and many local firms employ a skilled HR executive who is backed up by a team of qualified HR professionals. While those teams' depth of knowledge is not yet comparable to that found in the West, this is primarily because of the young age and inexperience of employees. But the trend is changing rapidly and the HR departments will soon be more like those found in the West.

MAKING IT WORK IN CHINA

*"Mighty are the great trends
of the world: those who go
with them flourish, those
who oppose them die."*
Sun Yat Sen

Introduction to Part II

The 11 chapters in this part are aimed at helping individual leaders do their work in China. While it was noted earlier that the primary audience for this work consists of those who are already familiar with China, the chapters are also valuable to newer leaders as a primer to leadership in China.

The part begins with a discussion of the dilemma between truth and courtesy in China. This is a source of conflict between Western and Chinese people, because of the greater focus on truth and directness in the West versus the need to be courteous and give "face" in China. The following chapter on trust notes the relatively longer time required to gain trust in China and the relative absence of the same kind of formal trust that we often find in Western firms among colleagues.

Chapter Eleven looks at the tricky dichotomy between empowerment and hierarchy. Most Western leaders arrive in China believing that they can empower their employees. Oftentimes, they find this is difficult to achieve in China and may be puzzled as to why. Most of the time, the reason is that the leader does not know how to integrate this best Western practice within a Confucian hierarchical system. Chapter Eleven examines this dilemma in detail.

This is followed by a chapter that examines the principle of individualism, found in most Western countries, versus the collectivist approach dominant in China. While this is indeed changing, especially among the younger Chinese, the remnants of a collectivist mentality are still quite evident in China.

Chapter Thirteen looks at the rule of man, which is typical in China, versus the rule of law, which permeates most Western countries. This relative absence of a consistent legal system is very troublesome for many Western leaders and a reason for the failure of some.

Chapter Fourteen looks at the apparent lack of innovation in Chinese employees compared to those in the West. It examines how risk-taking is a potential source of fear among Chinese employees and needs to be carefully reinforced in order to help them become more innovative.

Decision-making is the subject of Chapter Fifteen. Leaders in China learn that the Western approach of "ready–fire–aim" is viewed very negatively in China, especially if an individual leader, and not a collective body of executives, does the firing. This chapter suggests ways to combine the Western and Eastern approaches to decision-making in order to satisfy Western bosses at home as well as Chinese workers in the firm.

Traditionally, Chinese leaders were not expected to help employees be motivated to perform according to any standards. In fact, employees in the past were suspicious of leaders who tried to motivate them as they felt the leader was only being self-serving. The idea of helping an employee to fulfill his or her own psychological–social needs through the firm is a Western one that needs to be explained in China before it can be understood by those whose motivation is at stake. Chapter Sixteen therefore examines how a leader in China can influence employee motivation.

The chapter on teamwork, Chapter Seventeen, is a logical follow-on from the previous one on motivation. But rather than focus on the individual, it focuses on how to get the best team performance from workers. The more subtle issue is how to get better cross-team collaboration from employees than what is commonly found in China.

Chapter Eighteen offers a very detailed look at reward program management in China. It examines base salary, incentive pay, and executive compensation, and describes not only how to lay out these programs in China but also how to use them strategically.

The final chapter in this second part of the book, on executive coaching in China, presents methods of giving individual leaders more personal help on matters that are aimed at making them better leaders. This is important in China because of the general belief that coaching is a remedial activity, rather than one aimed at accelerated growth.

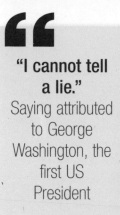

"I cannot tell a lie."
Saying attributed to George Washington, the first US President

Chapter 9

TRUTH VERSUS COURTESY

The Dilemma of Truth versus Courtesy in China

Both Chinese and Western cultures are truthful, and both are courteous. But Westerners are more direct and, therefore, more willing to get to the truth at the expense of courtesy. Chinese, on the other hand, are more likely to favor courtesy over truth if this approach allows everyone to save face. Again, I can take from my experience at my prior firm in Beijing. As head of the firm, I needed to know everything I could about our company and the competition. With a weak knowledge of the language, I was totally dependent on my staff to let me know what was happening so that I could react accordingly. But I was almost always the last one to know when the news was bad. If a competitor won a project, I needed to probe to find this out. (In the US, I would have been flooded with emails.) If someone was leaving the firm, especially to join a competitor, neither the employee nor his or her supervisor would confide in me about the fact. There was usually some excuse about the employee going to graduate school or leaving to travel abroad. A few weeks after the person left, I would learn that he or she was now working for a competitor. Then I would learn that everyone else knew this, but that they had not wanted me to feel too bad about it so they had kept it from me.

I was not the only leader to be in that position. Patrick Huang of Watson Wyatt describes a similar situation.

> *"We had an employee who decided to resign from the firm. He told us that his parents wanted him to go back to his hometown and prepare for his MBA. He convinced everyone about his loyalty to our firm and his desire to return after he obtained his MBA. He even sent an email to everyone on the China staff to let us know that this was his favorite consulting firm and that if he ever re-joined the world of consulting, he would come back to Watson Wyatt. About two weeks after he sent the email, we learned that he was now employed at a competitor."*
>
> **Patrick Huang**, Managing Director, Watson Wyatt Worldwide, Shanghai, China.

Someone pointed out to me that this kind of behavior is considered quite normal and not necessarily bad. After all, the person wanted to be kind and to make it very clear how grateful he was to have worked at Watson Wyatt and how he thought well of the firm. Even though he may have known that he would be joining a competing firm, his intention was simply to say nice things about his current firm and to give everyone "face." The fact that he was joining the other firm was something that would happen later but should not interfere with his kind comments about his current firm.

Western leaders may become frustrated in China with this focus on courtesy over sharing important information. Likewise, Chinese leaders are often frustrated by the expectations of foreign employees and their foreign headquarters to know quickly what is happening, regardless of the impact on "face."

"Face" (面子, *mian zi*) in Chinese has a broader meaning than in the West. While most people in the world want to keep their reputation clean and maintain their self-respect, the Chinese are particularly smitten with this concept. Leaders use middlemen (中间人, *zhong jian ren*) much more often than Westerners, primarily to engage in matters that could potentially threaten the "face" of the leader or the other party.

This issue of favoring courtesy over truth is also a reason that some Chinese leaders are accused of being vague in their responses to others. As noted in an earlier chapter, one Chinese colleague told me that she and her colleagues played a guessing game at work to determine the true meaning of their boss's statements.

Some Chinese employees have a tough time with their Western bosses who favor truth over courtesy. On the truth side, Western leaders are often open to suspicion. Chinese employees also try to guess if there is a hidden meaning in a statement, even when the Western boss is simply stating what he or she views as a straightforward fact. On the courtesy side (which is often viewed by the Chinese as a lack thereof), Westerners are often criticized by their Chinese employees for coming to the point too directly, even at the expense of causing someone to lose face.

Gao Yong of Career International makes a point about this.

> *"Westerners can be a bit more direct than the Chinese. We tend to keep some of our ideas to ourselves. Therefore, it is sometimes more difficult to understand the true meaning of what a Chinese person says. For 5,000 years, this has been a family-owned and family-run country. Now that it is so much more complicated, people are afraid to say too much to others. Other families might have secrets that they don't want to share. Very few of us are very direct and open. We have to be careful in our choice of words."*
>
> **Gao Yong,** President, Career International, Inc., Beijing, China.

The lesson for employees is that they always need to read meaning into the words they hear spoken. There is not just a suspicion that these words are guarded; there is an expectation that this is the case. That is why the directness of Westerners is both refreshing and confusing. Chinese people are relieved that they don't always have to guess their boss's meaning. On the other hand, until a strong level of trust is obtained, there may still be suspicion that there is more to the Western leader's words than what seems obvious. With a Chinese leader, employees pretty much expect that they will need to guess. With Westerners, employees need to guess about what was said and whether it is necessary then also to guess the hidden meaning.

Ren Binyan of Alcoa puts this issue in a positive light.

"The more educated the person, the more sophisticated he or she is. These people are more concerned with not wanting to hurt your feelings. So, rather than do so, I may not say it. This is cultural.

Also, Chinese people often do not volunteer to give advice, while Westerners commonly offer unsolicited advice. Sometimes, Chinese people see this as being too aggressive. A Chinese person might advise a Western colleague against something that might fail. If the Westerner pushes back, the Chinese person would let go so the Westerner could test it himself or herself. But he would always be willing to help again if the Westerner asked for it."

Ren Binyan, *Vice President, Alcoa (China), Investment Company, Ltd., Beijing, China.*

The thrust of this concept is not about dishonesty, but more about the overriding importance of courtesy and saving face. To the Chinese, this is one of the most important values. It is certainly more important than just passing along facts that could be harmful to the listener.

How to Handle the Issue of Truth versus Courtesy in China

So, what is one to do? If you are a leader in China and value truthfulness more highly than courtesy, how do you get employees to be more forthcoming in their dealings? Here are a few suggestions:

- Be very clear with subordinates about what you (the leader) expect. If you want to know if a contract was lost as soon as the others know, tell people that it is your expectation that you be kept promptly informed as well. Let them know that if someone holds back this information, you will consider it a dereliction of duty.
- Explain how getting accurate information has a huge impact on your success. I like to use the analogy of the airline pilot who flies above the clouds and needs the information that comes from the dials and meters in the cockpit. Without that accurate information, the airplane will crash. The same goes for the company.

Senior employees are like these dials and meters. In fact, you can use the "face" issue to explain that if something important happens and you do not know about it in time, you will lose much face at your headquarters. Most Chinese employees will understand this analogy and see the relative value in revealing the truth here, rather than rely on old habits that could cause you to lose face with your bosses.

- Select one or two key confidantes whom you can count on for information. In my case, there was one person on my team who tried to protect my "face" by letting me know in advance when something was brewing. She was still embarrassed and apologetic when she gave me bad news. I knew it was difficult for her. But she did it, and I appreciated it and reinforced this very helpful behavior whenever I could.
- Don't be disappointed! This concept of favoring courtesy over truth is very old in China and will take a long time to change completely, especially among older employees. But have patience and allow occasional slips. If you regularly reinforce the importance of receiving accurate and timely information, you will eventually get it.

Now let us look at the other side of the matter. Suppose there is a leader in the organization (either Western or Chinese) who goes too far in the direction of truth over courtesy. That is, the leader is so concerned with getting the message out in a direct fashion, that people regularly lose face. If I were coaching this leader, I would make the following suggestions:

- What is your intention? Do you just want to communicate bad news, or do you have another motive related to the employee with whom you are communicating?
- Is there an alternative method for getting this information out that will not cause someone to feel embarrassed or ashamed? For example, if someone has truly done something wrong, can you give this feedback in a corrective way and not use negative terms that may cause one to feel like a personal failure? This is particularly important in China, given the importance of saving face.
- If the leader is Western, I would point out in my coaching the way a Chinese person may receive the news. Even though

the intention might have been relatively harmless, the perception could be disastrous.

- If the leader is Chinese, they can be reminded of the Confucian principle quoted at the beginning of the previous chapter: "What you do not wish upon yourself, do not do unto others." In my experience, many Chinese leaders have not been trained in the "softer" side of people management. Concepts such as empathy are not well understood in China. Many people do not realize the impact of their statements. They may think they are being corrective, when in fact they are being negative.

The issue of pitting truth against courtesy affects everyone in Chinese businesses. As a leader, you need to balance both. Truth is necessary to run the organization, but so is courtesy with employees. The new China leader is required to do both.

Another matter that is closely related to this one is trust. We will examine this issue in the next chapter.

Chapter Nine Executive Summary

Truth versus Courtesy

- Chinese and Western cultures are both truthful and courteous. But Westerners are more direct and therefore more willing to get to the truth at the expense of courtesy. Chinese, on the other hand, are more likely to favor courtesy and face-saving at the expense of truth.

- Western leaders often are frustrated in China by the focus on courtesy over truth. Likewise, Chinese leaders are often frustrated by the expectations of foreign employees and their foreign headquarters to know quickly what is happening, regardless of the impact on "face."

- Face-saving has a deeper meaning in China than in the West, and many Chinese will go to great lengths either to save their own or someone else's "face." That is why many Chinese will sacrifice the truth in order to help their leader save face, even though the leader prefers to know the truth as soon as others know it.

- Dealing with this dilemma in China depends on whether people are favoring truth or courtesy. In the former case, a leader needs to make it clear to others the importance of knowing the facts as soon as possible. He or she also needs to indicate how important it is to running a successful operation that information be made available promptly and accurately. In the latter case, a leader needs to learn the impact of being too direct at the expense of courtesy, especially in China. Causing an employee to feel shame as a result of the way information is presented will not go down very well in China, as other employees will be fearful of the same happening to them. This tends to lead to a passive and non-risk-taking workforce.

- Leaders in China need to find the right balance between truth and courtesy, and encourage employees to use both in a harmonious way. Favoring one exclusively over the other will cause the company to fail.

Chapter 10

TRUST

One of the best comparisons of how "trust" varies around the world was written by Francis Fukuyama of Johns Hopkins University in the US.[1] In his definition, he refers to trust as "the expectation that arises within a community of regular, honest, and co-operative behavior."[2] He believes that trust is required in a company for the business leader and other employees to work well together. He describes the Chinese, in relation to business, as having a more difficult time than Westerners in becoming corporate professional managers because of their inclination to trust deeply only those people with whom they have a very close relationship. Likewise, the Chinese are likely to mistrust people outside of their family or close inner group. Based on these observations, Fukuyama identified China as a "low-trust" society.[3]

> *"In China, we are very slow to trust others. Do you know how hard it is to make close friends here? If you did not go to school with the person, you just don't know them well enough to have strong trust right away. We go out together a lot. We drink together and tell stories about our lives. Sometimes we laugh and sometimes we fight. Over time, we begin to have trust.*
>
> *Westerners usually will not do this. They want to get right down to business. We have a saying, 'Xian jiao peng you hou zuo sheng yi.'* (先交朋友，后做生意, *first make friends and then do business.*)
>
> *(continued)*

(*continued*)

But I have to say, this is changing in China. Companies realize the importance of moving quickly. So they sometimes sacrifice getting the stronger relationship that they know they should have in order to get going. I'm not sure this is a good thing, but it is the way we are heading. That comes from the West."

Gao Yong, *President, Career International, Inc., Beijing, China.*

Romie Littrell wrote of trust in China: "The collectivist mentality tends to treat strangers as meaningless objects or as objects to be taken advantage of. ... People whom one does not know ... are outsiders, to whom one owes no obligation."[4] He also described how Chinese managers in one of his studies were at first reluctant to participate for fear they would be "punished" for giving negative ratings to their own managers. This, he concluded, indicated a strong lack of trust.[5]

In order to move quickly in business today, there is often not enough time to establish *guan xi* (关系, very close, long-term, reciprocal relationships) or to follow the habit of *ren qing* (人情, the granting and receiving of favors to reinforce *guan xi*).

"Trust is built up over time. People talk about trust here, but in reality, Chinese people do not start as trusting souls. We need to learn to trust someone. We need to see your behavior first. We will give you plenty of respect, but we hold back our trust until we see the behavior that backs up your words. I think many Westerners are more willing to accept your words first and trust you until you prove yourself unworthy of it. We Chinese need to form the trust before we accept someone's words."

Yi Min, *Director of Global Leadership and Organization Development, Lenovo Group, Raleigh, North Carolina, United States.*

In an earlier chapter, I referred to the distinction Nandani Lynton made between the "formal trust" found in many Western companies and the deeper, "personal trust" required in China.[6] Let me quickly restate that difference. Formal trust is what allows many people in the West to quickly trust others who work in their company to engage in transactions that are required to move the company in a certain direction. The assumption is that these others with whom you have formal trust will share the same business goals and values and it is therefore safe to proceed. If you require the deeper form of trust, "personal trust," you will be hampered in your progress and perhaps not move as quickly as those in work cultures where formal trust is evident.

Another issue related to the relative lack of trust in China is how foreigners are viewed. When I hear some of my Chinese colleagues refer to foreigners, I detect an element of superiority that I do not often pick up in the West. The formal word for "foreigner" in Chinese is *wai guo ren* (外国人), which can be literally translated as "foreign country person." But the more common expression for a foreigner is *lao wai* (老外). This term has two meanings: "foreigner" and "layman." This is a *double entendre*, which could imply that the foreigner is not as senior as a Chinese person. This is not to imply that foreigners, especially those who have lived and worked in China for a long time, are not given plenty of respect. In fact, the respect level that I have found in China is much higher than I would expect elsewhere. But words like *lao wai* seem to contain an element of judgment that does not exist in the English word "foreigner," which simply means "from another country."

China is a country that has long been embattled. It has probably been invaded and occupied by foreign armies as much as anywhere else in the world. As such, it is understandable that the Chinese may historically have been wary of foreigners. I make these points about foreigners in this chapter to illustrate that, if you are a foreigner, it is even more difficult to gain trust in China than if you are Chinese.

Recent Chinese History

One need not go too far back in history to understand why the Chinese continue to be suspicious of others and are relatively less trustful than Westerners. During the Cultural Revolution, which gripped China from the mid-1960s to the mid-1970s, it was difficult to trust anyone. Friends reported on friends, children told on their parents, and sometimes even spouses reported their better half to the local authorities for violating one or another form of expected behavior. In many cases, the consequences of this behavior were severe. People lost their jobs, their status, and sometimes their lives. It is understandable, then, that a society with such a recent history would encourage people to be very careful about whom they trust. As a Chinese friend of mine recently told me: "It is very difficult to form a true, new friendship in China. We always hold back a little of ourselves. We are not so willing to give all of ourselves away, for fear of being exposed in some way."

I believe this also explains why it is often difficult to extend trust among employees in a company. A simple request by one employee may be met with doubts and questions such as "Why do you want that?". Rather than giving a simple "yes" or "no" answer, there is often the suspicion among employees that your intentions are suspect and so, rather than expose themselves to the danger, they will sometimes not comply with your requests.

Also related to this is the need for some employees to "guess" what is intended by a manager's instructions. I mentioned in the previous chapter that it is considered a corporate core competency in some Chinese firms (especially SOEs) not to ask too many questions. Instead, the competent employee will properly guess the manager's intentions. By intentionally being vague, the manager does not expose himself too much. By guessing correctly, the employee does a good job without causing the manager to reveal too much.

This kind of behavior is not easy for Westerners to understand and may cause them to accuse the Chinese of being evasive and even unsure of themselves. While I do not believe that to be the case, I understand the Western concern and see how this can lead to misunderstandings between the two. In multinational firms, where Chinese and Western employees work side by side, this can be a common cause of friction.

Until Chinese and Western employees are able to see eye-to-eye on the subtle meaning of trust in China, there will be breakdowns in communication. This will slow things down and prevent companies from moving ahead as quickly as they should.

"I am very proud to be Chinese. But the issue of trust and truthfulness here is one that concerns me very much. Sometimes, a leader will pay a compliment to someone that I know is not true. It is just made to give the person 'face.' I know that Westerners do this, too, but not as much as the Chinese. When someone pays me a compliment here, I wonder if it is a true compliment."

Janet Zhong, Vice President, Human Resources, Alcoa (China) Investment Company Ltd., Asia Pacific, Beijing, China.

How to Deal with the Relatively Low Level of Trust in China

How is a leader to deal with the relatively low level of trust in China? How does one gain the trust necessary to lead the company to success? How does the leader know whom he or she can trust?

The first thing to realize about trust in China is that it is difficult to gain. It does not simply come with the job. My recommendation to new leaders in China is to be sure to accomplish the specific things that you promise. We have a saying in the US, "Under-promise and over-deliver." I believe this advice will work well in China in order to gain trust. Nothing will cause you to fail more quickly than over-promising and under-delivering. Unfortunately, many Westerners do just this. Chinese often attribute this to the desire by Westerners to make themselves heroes. I observed a new Western leader make this mistake recently in China. He continually talked about the new business he would generate for the firm. At first, the other employees were excited about these new opportunities. After a time, however, when nothing had happened, the employees became suspicious. As the employer continued to make speeches about all the good that would come of his work, he lost the trust of all his employees. He left the firm after a very short time. This kind of behavior will be unsuccessful in any culture, but in China, it can lead to disaster. If you want to gain trust, you must deliver on your promises.

Second, I recommend that you start by trying to gain formal trust, rather than expecting that you can instantaneously gain personal trust. Let us take a look at what some leaders in China have been doing to gain trust.

> *"To gain trust takes longer here. You need to start a new relationship with everyone. You are guilty until proven innocent. People are bound by their earlier relationships and obligations. You need to listen very carefully. You need to understand when someone is saying 'yes' but really meaning 'no.' I think I have built comfortable trust relationships with my senior team in China, but it has taken a long time with lots of give and take. The trust is still developing. I try to regularly inform, include, and enable."*
>
> **Hala Helmy,** *President, Mundipharma, Beijing, China.*

Many Western leaders who are new in China expect that their colleagues will trust them immediately. The idea that people from the same firm might be doubtful about your trustworthiness is alien to most Westerners. In an earlier chapter on Western culture, I mentioned that trust in others is a core Western value. Westerners arrive in China with this expectation. It is not that they are naïve. Most new leaders understand that they must perform to gain respect, but they are not ready for mistrust.

Victor Lang of MMD Asia Pacific talks about how he tries to gain trust from his colleagues.

> *"I do two things to gain the trust of my employees. First, I try to show my sincerity by working very hard. My cell phone is on 24 hours a day, seven days a week. When employees see me make such a sacrifice, it has a great impact. Second, I take pains to choose my own staff. I find that handpicking staff breeds loyalty and trust. When I go away on business, I do not worry about these people as I might if we lacked trust."*
>
> **Victor Lang,** *President, MMD Asia Pacific, Ltd., Beijing, China.*

This comment has two significant messages. The first is that trust needs to be gained by performance. But the second message is also very telling. The fact that Mr. Lang sees the need to bring in his own people says something important about trust in China. It underscores the aforementioned difference between China and the West regarding trust. It is not a given in China that good performance alone will guarantee trust. If you want to assure yourself of trust in China, it might be necessary to bring in your own "trusted" staff.

Kelly Wang of GW Technologies makes a related point.

> *"I believe the best way to get trust in your company is to hire people with similar values. If you trust the people you hire, they are more likely to trust you. Our environment is very open. People are willing to talk about anything, including their mistakes. I try to lead from my heart, not from my head. Hiring the right people, having an open environment, and leading from your heart are all the things that lead to trust."*
>
> **Kelly Wang,** *Founder and Director, GW Technologies Co., Ltd., Beijing, China.*

I have a few more suggestions aimed mostly at Westerners. First, be willing to talk about yourself. Chinese employees will be curious about your background. Tell people about your history, your family, your hometown, your educational experiences, and your business experiences. This will allow others to see you more personally and assess your willingness to share. These things breed trust.

Second, follow the Chinese business custom of socializing after work. This is not all that common in the West. Employees may socialize informally in the West, but the leader is often only part of formal events such as Christmas parties and annual picnics. While those are also good ways to build trust, the Chinese will more commonly expect their bosses to sometimes let their hair down with them. This also allows employees to see the human side of their leader, which they really need to see if they are to trust them.

In the next chapter, we move on to a very common phenomenon that is often a surprise to Westerners. This is the difficulty they may encounter when trying to empower employees.

Notes

1 Francis Fukuyama, *Trust: The Social Virtues and the Creation of Prosperity* (New York: Free Press, 1995).
2 *Ibid.*, p. 26.
3 *Ibid.*
4 Romie Littrell, "Desirable Leadership Behaviors of Multi-Cultural Managers in China," *Journal of Management Development*, Vol. 21, No. 1, 2002, pp. 5–74 at p. 27.
5 *Ibid.*, p. 30.
6 Nandani Lynton, "Challenges for the Chinese Executive," *Thunderbird*, Fall 2006, pp. 39–41 at p. 41.

Chapter Ten Executive Summary

Trust

- Both external experts and local business leaders define China as a low-trust society. The implication for leadership is that Chinese people will be slow to trust their leaders.

- We can distinguish between the formal trust that comes from being a part of the same company, evident in the West, and personal trust, which is required in China. Since personal trust takes longer to obtain, Chinese companies are at a disadvantage. Therefore, this is a bigger challenge for leaders in Chinese companies than for those in the West.

- The Chinese are typically more wary of foreigners than local nationals are in other countries, especially in the West. As such, if you are a Western leader working in China, the trust challenge may be more difficult than for a Chinese leader working in China.

- China has a long history of being overrun by outside conquerors. Recent history also has led people to be suspicious of others. During the Cultural Revolution, few people could be trusted. One needed to be very careful about what one did or said, even with members of one's own family. Today, while these kinds of issues no longer exist, the culture is still embedded with these suspicions.

- Many current business leaders in China have been able to overcome some of these suspicions and have generated trust among their workforce. Tactics have included delivering on your promises, creating an open work environment, talking openly about themselves and their families, socializing after work, hiring people with similar values, and leading from one's heart rather than just from one's head.

> "There is order when the king is king, the minister is minister, the father is father, and the son is son."
> Confucius

> "Just call me Bob."
> A typical statement by an American CEO to his staff

Chapter 11

EMPOWERMENT VERSUS HIERARCHY

Empowerment is a given in the West. Every Western leadership book talks about its importance in best leveraging your team and getting the most value from your employees. Therefore, whenever Western leadership experts come to China to speak about leadership, they bring up the subject of empowerment, explaining its importance and describing how to implement an empowerment culture.

Many Chinese leaders understand the value of empowerment. But they also understand that it is not as easily achieved in China as in the West. Westerners generally want to be empowered, because it fosters their wish to be independent and to "own" their jobs. Confucian doctrine, however, espouses order and respect for authority. The quotation at the beginning of this chapter implies that for there to be order, people need to understand their place in society. Granting empowerment to a Chinese person who is rooted in Confucianism may be downright unsettling.

This is also true in business. Empowerment upsets the order between the leader and the follower. There are legends in Chinese folklore about people who were killed for violating the proper hierarchy. John Graham and Mark Lam describe the case of Cheng

Han-cheng and his wife. Cheng's wife beat her mother-in-law. This violation of order was considered such a severe crime that both the wife and her husband were skinned alive, "their flesh displayed at the gates of various cities, and their bones burned to ashes. Neighbors and extended family were also punished."[1] This story is known by most Chinese. It helps everyone understand the importance of roles in China.

I doubt that Chinese workers fear for their lives when their Western boss tries to empower them, but I know that they are confused. In fact, to some Confucian purists, violating this order between the boss and the follower can be considered immoral.

> *"Empowerment is still a problem here in China. We are so used to having a hierarchy. It is safer for me. I have my job, and my boss has his job. If you empower me and I make a mistake, I can be blamed. Chinese people don't like to be blamed. We can be responsible for the work we do, but we usually don't want to be 'empowered' to take on something new because of the fear of failure. Nevertheless, we need to do this more in China. We need a system for empowering employees because the middle levels keep getting cut in our organizations and someone has to take up the work that used to be done there. The key for the leader will be to find the right balance between empowering others and doing the work themselves."*
>
> **Yi Min**, *Director of Global Leadership and Organization Development, Lenovo Group, Raleigh, North Carolina, United States.*

These comments by Yi Min refer to the second theme of the book, which is that one cannot simply import best Western leadership practices into China and expect them to work. As common as the concept of empowerment is in the West, it certainly requires modification before it can be applied in China.

Xu Fang of TCL Corporation has a great deal to say about this subject.

"This is such a complicated subject in China. In ancient times, leaders would use empowerment for political reasons. If something was potentially difficult, the leader would pass the job onto one of his underlings. It was more a matter of manipulation than motivation. So this led Confucius to make his famous statement about order—'there is order when the king is king, the minister is minister, the father is father, and the son is son.'

Nowadays, the hierarchy in business is not as rigid as it used to be. We needed to move away from this hierarchical approach in order to free up the leaders to be more strategic and to allow the employees to do more of the less strategic work.

But this is causing some confusion. For example, at TCL, our Chairman believes in this concept and espoused it when the company was formed. But some of the employees mistook this to mean 'just do it.' As such, they would sometimes do things very incorrectly because they did not encompass the idea that empowerment did not mean total individual freedom. It still required them to follow company guidelines and to follow best practices.

It was also difficult for some of our other leaders who also did not understand when to empower. Sometimes, the employee they were empowering was really not yet capable of doing what they were being asked to do.

The bottom line is that it is now working, but it has taken a lot of explanation and trial and error to get to this point."

Xu Fang, *Vice President, TCL Institute of Leadership Development, TCL Corporation, Huizhou, China.*

As this comment describes, empowerment can work well in China, but it needs to be introduced to all parties in a way that fully explains what it is and what it is intended to be used for. Otherwise, it has the potential to be misunderstood and may be abused.

Gao Yong of Career International adds to the discussion of empowerment.

> *"This is still a new concept for us in China. Sometimes leaders are reluctant to empower too much. Business ethics are not very developed yet. Laws are still not very clear. A Chinese leader might be reluctant to give away too much power through 'empowerment' for fear of that power being used against him. It is safer not to empower too much."*
>
> **Gao Yong,** *President, Career International Inc., Beijing, China.*

Obviously, empowerment in China is easier said than done. As the prior comments by Chinese leaders describe, it cannot simply be introduced as many Western books describe. Rather, the leader needs to understand empowerment within the context of Chinese culture.

Let us examine some ways of dealing with this conflict between empowerment and hierarchy.

How to Deal with the Conflict between Empowerment and Hierarchy in China

The best way I know of making empowerment work in China is to begin by introducing it gradually and in discrete steps. First, the leader needs to explain very clearly that he or she expects the employee to take independent action. The leader will provide general direction about what needs to be done, but it is expected that the employee will then decide how best to execute the order. The leader also needs to explain that it is okay to ask questions and to make a mistake. There is no penalty for making a mistake if the employee is trying something new and innovative. After this clear explanation, the leader needs to test how much empowerment will work with each employee. Some employees in China jump at the chance to be empowered and do not worry at all about the hierarchy, as long as they are assured by the boss that it is acceptable to do things this way. But many others will be reluctant to go too far without specific direction. For that reason, the skillful leader will implement these changes slowly and carefully.

In my experience, with newer and younger employees, it is best for the leader to "check in" from time to time to see how things are progressing. Many of these employees will not admit to having a problem for fear of appearing weak or incompetent. This is where the leader can check to ensure that the employee is on the right path and making progress. As noted earlier, this is a gradual process. Take your time. Reinforce the message regularly that you expect the employee to work independently and without too much specific direction from you. This will save everyone time and also allow the employee to do the job in the way that he or she believes is best.

In a discussion on this subject with Li Yong, the Director of Leadership Consulting for Mercer China, he recommended using the term "delegation," rather than "empowerment," at least as an intermediate step. The idea is that delegation, unlike empowerment, doesn't connote ownership. Chinese employees may be more comfortable with this term, as they have responsibility for doing the job, but don't have to own all of the results. With delegation, the leader is still the owner. Then, once the employee is more comfortable, the leader can change to a purer empowerment approach.[2]

Kelly Wang of GW Technologies stresses the need for clear lines of authority for empowerment to work. But he also adds a few words of caution.

"Empowerment works in my company because we have very clear lines of authority. For example, functional managers have very liberal payment-approving authority. As long as they stick within their budgets and get the job done, they are empowered to spend as they see fit. We do have many clear regulations so we can give people lots of power if they follow the regulations. Sometimes people make mistakes, but that is almost always tolerated. You can't expect people to be empowered and then punish them if they make mistakes. For junior hires, we expect them to follow the rules pretty closely. But for someone who will lead a functional area, we look to hire people who like to be empowered. We want them to be independent.

(continued)

(continued)

The concern in China, however, is that some employees might abuse their new power. We had to test this. We started with our core team and then began to empower others. So far, it is working fine."

Kelly Wang, *Founder and Director, GW Technologies Co. Ltd., Beijing, China.*

There are two more points to consider. Do not forget to explain to employees why you as a leader value empowerment and how it has been proven to be an effective approach. First of all, empowerment leads to the best results because it relies on the people closest to the work to resolve issues and get the job done. Secondly, empowerment provides more employee satisfaction than just telling people what to do. While this may not yet be a strong motivational need in China, it will be. Once employees get beyond their basic motivational needs in a firm, they will begin looking for more intrinsic rewards such as job satisfaction and job ownership. I will have more to say on this subject in a later chapter.

The second point is more complicated because it can be quite subtle. Chinese employees expect their leaders to be doers. I was providing executive coaching to a CEO in China. When I sought feedback from others in the firm about their assessments of the CEO's performance, I learned that several employees viewed his empowering style as a weakness. They believed that he needed to show more ability to do the jobs he was empowering others to do. In China, it is important for the CEO to display solid expertise and high levels of work competencies before he or she can expect followers to accept empowerment.

I once coached a very successful American leader who was having a huge problem with empowerment in China. He said that in the US, he could tell people what he expected to be done. Then, when he came back two or three weeks later, the job would be completed. If there were questions along the way, the workers would ask him. There was never a problem in getting the job done. In China, this did not happen for him. He would empower someone to do something.

The employee would agree and there would be no further questions. When he returned at the time agreed upon, there would have been no progress. This happened on several occasions, leading him to the (erroneous) conclusion that Chinese employees did not take their responsibilities as seriously as their Western counterparts. It took several months of coaching to show him first how empowerment was viewed in China. Second, he needed to see that he was being criticized by his employees for leaving such significant work with them, rather than owning it himself. Finally, he needed to see that a more gradual approach in China could bear much more fruit than the very direct Western approach of simply empowering someone to carry out an assignment, asking for questions, and then leaving them to get on with the job. Chinese employees expect their leaders to be much more hands-on and to respect the value of the hierarchy.

The trick with introducing empowerment is to do it in a balanced way. The most junior employees are not yet ready to be empowered. They need a lot of specific direction. The most senior employees may be confused by empowerment for the cultural reasons described above. Mid-level people who are ambitious and eager to succeed in the firm may be the best candidates for empowerment. But, as noted previously, the leader needs to provide clear explanations about why empowerment is valuable, what is specifically expected of the employee, and how he or she stands to benefit.

In the next chapter, we will examine a fundamental difference between Western and Chinese leaders: the issue of individualism versus collectivism.

Notes

1   John L. Graham and N. Mark Lam, "The Chinese Negotiation," *Harvard Business Review*, Vol. 81, No. 10, October 2003, pp. 82–91 at p. 84.

2   Interview with Li Yong, Mercer Human Resource Consulting, Beijing, January 9, 2007.

Chapter Eleven Executive Summary

Empowerment versus Hierarchy

- The Western concept of empowerment has been introduced to China without properly recognizing its inherent conflict with the Confucian notion of hierarchy. In order to introduce empowerment successfully in China, a leader needs to learn to integrate these disparate concepts.

- A secondary issue with empowerment in China is the concern of some Chinese leaders that employees may abuse their power. Chinese leaders are therefore sometimes reluctant to relinquish any control in the form of empowerment.

- Chinese employees sometimes see the empowering leader as "weak" for trying to hand off matters that they think he or she should own.

- The best way for a leader to introduce empowerment to a workforce is to do it gradually. This includes providing very clear explanations upfront of why it is being done, how it will work, and what is expected as an outcome.

- Try delegating before empowering. With delegating, you can shift responsibility for getting a job done, without actually transferring ownership as you do with empowerment. Chinese employees understand delegation much more easily than empowerment.

- Avoid empowering young and new employees until you feel they understand why you are empowering them and how it will help them do a better job and be more satisfied with their roles.

Chapter 12

INDIVIDUALISM VERSUS COLLECTIVISM

One of the best examples of the conflict between individualism and collectivism in China is this story by Ruby Chen of McKinsey.

"I had a private Chinese company client in China that merged with a Western firm. Both of these firms were successful and significant business leaders in their home countries. They came together with the best of intentions and a mutual desire to make the merger work. One of the things the Western firm recommended upfront was that they do a talent inventory to make sure that the best and the brightest employees from both firms are retained and rewarded.

This is a very individualistic idea. The Chinese firm insisted that their success was not really dependent on individuals, but rather on the strength of the teams. While it was true that many of the teams were dependent on certain individuals, it was more the case that the individuals were successful because of the strength of the collective nature of the teams.

While the merger is still considered successful and it seems that it will work out its intercultural differences, this talent matter is still not fully resolved. Both sides have come a long way in understanding the

(continued)

(continued)

other's views, but neither is fully convinced of the other's approach. To this day, they are compromising and trying to work this through. Fortunately, there is a mutual respect and a desire to work it out. But the fundamental difference between individualism and collectivism is predominant and has not yet allowed them to resolve this basic dilemma."

Ruby Chen, *Director of McKinsey Leadership Institute in China, Beijing, China.*

China has long been a family-run country. It has also been, and still is, primarily a rural nation. These two institutions, the family and the farm, are the core of China. Both the family and a rural environment are collectivist in nature. They depend on working together and aiming for harmony. When Mao Zedong came to power, he reinforced the collectivist view by eradicating landownership and individualism and sending nearly everyone to work in collectivist communes. Thus, China has been more collectivistic than individualistic in both its ancient and modern histories.

To be fair, there are many leaders in China today who believe that the days of collectivism in China will soon be gone.

"China is becoming less and less collectivistic. The people born after 1980, who we call 'ba ling hou' (八零后), are much more individualistic than collectivistic. In the cities, they are products of the 'one child policy.' Their parents have pampered them. Also, as China becomes more prosperous, the families have much more to give these young people. You will find that soon individualists will run China, just like in the West. It is only a matter of time."

Yi Min, *Director of Global Leadership and Organization Development, Lenovo Group, Raleigh, North Carolina, United States.*

Even if Yi Min is correct, and it is just a matter of time, the fact remains that China today is more collectivistic than individualistic.

Westerners coming to lead in China need to accommodate this reality. Anyone trying to stand out as in the West will be hammered down in China.

There are counters to this argument. Guo Xin of Mercer challenges the entire concept.

"The idea that China today is collectivist is a myth. It is true that many individuals choose not to go against the state today, but that is more to maintain stability than to further a collectivist mentality. We are becoming risk-takers and individualists more and more."

Guo Xin, *Managing Director, Greater China, Mercer Consulting, Beijing, China.*

But this is a view still held only by a minority. The majority of Chinese leadership experts who were interviewed for this book, as well as most of the literature on the subject, identify China as still being a collectivist society that is moving gradually toward individualism.

In a recent book on China, *China into the Future*, the authors contend that this gradual transition from collectivism to individualism is creating a serious problem for the Chinese Communist Party, as well as for individuals in society. "[T]here has been a transition from reliance on the collective to a belief in the individual. Socialism rests on the principle that the individual can derive more from the collective than he or she can by working alone. Markets place individual choices … at the center. This creates a problem for the Party as its ideology is based on the former premise and it cannot offer effective guidance in the new society. … For the individual, this contradiction creates confusions as official rhetoric bears little resemblance to reality as lived on the streets."[1]

My own observation is that, while the prediction that collectivism is changing to individualism in China is valid, there are still many signs of collectivism that one would not see in the West. The vast size of China's population requires a collectivist mentality just to get along. Individualists could not crowd onto buses the way commuters do in Beijing. Individualists could not travel in crowded subway cars the way they do in Shanghai. Sure, Chinese people complain about these things (and perhaps those complaints are a sign of the transition to individualism), but they tolerate them. Westerners have a very difficult time with these realities. When forced, they too comply, but generally they handle them less well than their Chinese counterparts.

When I first arrived in China, I was taken to a restaurant where, after dinner, musical entertainment was offered. People danced in a large group at the tables. There were no apparent dance partners, as one would usually find in the West. Rather, everyone danced as part of the group, and seemed to both fit into, and get lost in, the collective.

So, even though we may be moving away from a collectivist mindset in China, there are still many remnants of this in people's attitudes, especially among older citizens. In business leadership, this fact has strong implications.

Dealing with the Individualist–Collectivist Dichotomy in China

The story by Ruby Chen that opens this chapter is one example of how Western leaders in China will face this problem. The focus on the team over the individual is an important difference from the West. The lesson for a leader is to ensure that his or her focus is on the team, as well as on specific individuals. Westerners also need to be reminded to give credit to the team, rather than take it themselves, as many Chinese claim Westerners are quick to do. In the book, *China CEO*, the authors quote Tang Jun, then President of Microsoft China. To paraphrase, he said that as a leader in China, if you present yourself humbly "as part of the team," you establish the type of support you need to get the job done. If you follow a typical Western approach, where the leader is supreme, you are more likely to fail.[2]

In a collectivist society, a company becomes like a family; that is, the employee becomes a part of something very important. He or she will be loyal to that entity and expect the same in return. Of course, this is less true in China today than during the time of the "iron rice bowl," when everyone who joined a company saw it as a mutually beneficial, lifelong relationship. But again, although this concept no longer rings true in China, there are still remnants of the idea, especially among older workers. The lesson for the leader, be he or she Western or Chinese, is to understand and respect the history of this collectivist employer–employee relationship. You cannot go wrong if you overplay this idea. You stand to fail only if you underplay it.

In the next chapter, we will examine another Western–Chinese dichotomy: the rule of law versus the rule of man.

Notes

1   W. John Hoffmann and Michael J. Enright (eds.), *China into the Future* (Singapore: John Wiley & Sons (Asia), 2008).
2   Juan Antonio Fernandez and Laurie Underwood, *China CEO: Voices of Experience* (Singapore: John Wiley & Sons (Asia), 2006).

Chapter Twelve Executive Summary

Individualism versus Collectivism

- Since China is historically both a family-run and a rural country, the theme of collectivism is strong. Unlike Western culture, which breeds individualists, Chinese culture breeds collectivists.

- Chinese collectivist culture has been changing and some predict it will not be long before individualists run China, just as they do in the West today.

- Business leaders need to recognize the history of collectivism in China and understand how it impacts a company. For example, there is a stronger emphasis on the team in China than on the individual workers. Secondly, the company has a history of providing a long-term relationship between the employees and the firm. While both of these practices are rapidly changing, especially among younger workers, the remnants of collectivism remain, even if only ideologically. The business leader needs to recognize this and heed its implications. Failure to do so can result in an unsuccessful leadership reign.

> "Lead the people with administrative injunctions and put them in their place with penal law, and they will avoid punishments but will be without a sense of shame. Lead them with excellence and put them in their place through roles and ritualistic practices, and in addition to developing a sense of shame, they will order themselves harmoniously."
>
> Confucius

Chapter 13

THE RULE OF MAN VERSUS THE RULE OF LAW

The Confucian saying that opens this chapter is very telling about China today. The idea is that if a government puts too many laws and regulations in place, the people will behave according to the law, but not according to any moral mandate. If we minimize our regulating, people will be forced to act according to their sense of what is right, rather than what is legal. In principle, that sounds pretty good. In reality, this approach has become a mess in China, especially for businesses. There is very little case law to guide companies. As such, people tend to interpret things as they see fit. This leads to long bouts of haggling among adversaries. It is an inefficient and slow process.

In the West, the law is very mature. There are, for the most part, clear directions for companies based on prior legal decisions. In China, the legal system is still relatively immature. Also, in China, the various government entities (provincial, county, and local) may have very different interpretations of the laws mandated by the state. Many argue that these interpretations are often self-serving and driven by those who have the most to lose if a particular regulation is followed.

Contracts

Let us look at one example: written contracts. In all Western countries where there is a "rule of law," the contract is a final document that cannot be violated without penalty. Only if both parties agree in writing that the contract needs to be changed can one party decide not to do something spelled out in the contract. In China, the contract often has a different meaning. It is more like what Westerners call a "letter of intent." That is, the contract can identify what is intended by both parties at a particular point in time. Both parties then move forward with that document as a guideline for how to proceed, but it is not always considered a final and permanent document. These very different views often cause conflict when there are relations between Chinese and Western managers.

In the West, since a contract is binding, people and organizations trust that if such a document exists, both parties will do all they can to honor it. The contract document is backed up by the signatures of both parties and, if necessary, by the courts of the land. The Western expectation is that a contract spells out exactly what both parties will do for the other, often including very specific payment terms. For the Chinese, such a document is neither considered binding nor backed up by any law. It is intended to be vague so that the parties can continue to negotiate and work out issues along the way. "When problems arise in contracts, Chinese expect them to be worked out as one human being to another."[1]

In the West, if one party cannot honor its part of the agreement, it must pay some form of compensation to the other party to make up for not doing what it said it would do. In Chinese culture, however, if there is a problem with the agreement, both parties will often work things out informally until there is a new agreement.

This new agreement, in turn, may again be changed. Chinese business people understand this difference between China and the West and try to accommodate Westerners when, inevitably, there are conflicts. But generally, the Chinese still often want to renegotiate agreements as the situation dictates. As such, many Western businessmen believe that their Chinese counterparts are violating agreements already decided upon and are therefore not trustworthy.

During the time I spent as head of a consulting company, this matter arose often and was a cause of great frustration. But I was not alone. Patrick Huang describes a typical experience.

> *"Earlier this year, we had a signed contract with a person who was to become an employee in three months. I regularly checked with him over that time to make sure he would still come. On the weekend before he was to start, I took him to dinner to re-confirm our contract and review the terms. He was pleasant and agreeable to everything.*
>
> *Two days later, on the Monday when he was to start work, he called me to say that he would not be coming after all. His company made a counter-offer that he accepted.*
>
> *What could I do? I guess I could have tried to sue him but I am doubtful that it would have been worth the time and cost.*
>
> *In my view, the contract was worthless. Basically, it was no more than a document for us to state our intent at one point in time."*
>
> **Patrick Huang**, *Managing Director, Watson Wyatt Worldwide, Shanghai, China.*

Some Chinese would argue that the very litigious Western system causes more delay than the Chinese system, which is not bogged down by numerous regulations. In the West, they say, lawyers get rich trying cases that could more easily be handled by a wise judge or a tribunal. The Chinese process requires less time, money, and effort, they argue. While this may sometimes be true, it is extremely confusing for businesses in China that have to go through such processes each time a matter comes up, even if it were handled before and there was a formal judgment.

The Legal System

Another example of the difference in law between China and the West is the basic premises of the two legal systems. In the West, you are presumed innocent until proven guilty. In other words, the law trusts that you are not guilty of a crime and it is up to the state to prove otherwise. In China, just the opposite is true. Once you are arrested, it is first presumed that you are guilty. The burden is on you to prove your innocence.

This presents a serious problem for companies that are often the subjects of legal complaints from embittered employees or local officials. Once the accusation is made, the burden is on the company to prove its innocence. Leaders need to be careful not to be too glib about an outcome, however much they believe in their innocence. As pointed out by John Hoffman and Michael Enright, "While the rules and regulations are becoming clearer over time, how they are interpreted and enforced is still subject to great uncertainty and potential inconsistency over time and place."[2]

Interviewing and Hiring Candidates

In most Western countries, an employer cannot discriminate against an employee or potential employee based on their race, color, religion, gender, or age. This ruling is even embedded in the hiring practice, where it is illegal during an interview to ask certain questions that are commonly asked in China. For example, a Chinese firm may want to know a candidate's age. It is perfectly acceptable to ask for this information during an interview. In many Western countries, it is illegal to ask this question, as the person may then not be hired because they are considered to be too old or too young. This is considered a form of illegal discrimination in many Western countries.

In China, the answers to these questions are very important in the decision of whether or not to hire someone. Most airlines and five-star hotels in China will only hire people whom they consider to be attractive in appearance and who are within their required age limits. There are also often interview questions related to one's patriotism. These are common practices and lawful questions in China. While some Western leaders may personally disapprove of such questions, it would be foolhardy to try to change them at this point in time. Unless the leader is trying to make a social point that is irrelevant to his or her success as a leader, there is no practical business reason to try and change this current practice.

Dealing with Conflicts between the Rule of Law and the Rule of Man

Hoffman and Enright spell out nicely the dilemma as it is viewed today. "Fundamentally, there is little middle ground between a judicial system that represents the interests of the Party and elite and one that is truly independent, making decisions and building case histories on objective decisions based on statute books."[3]

While most Westerners view this as a problem, Lenovo's Yi Min has an interesting twist on this apparent conflict. She sees this dichotomy as an entrepreneurial opportunity. She describes Lenovo's founder, Liu Chuanzhi.

> *"Liu Chuanzhi was very entrepreneurial when it came to the legal system in China. He knew that it was immature and he needed to be flexible when interpreting some of the mandates that were passed on. He had the guts to break some rules because he felt he was right to do so, but he was prepared to bear the consequences if he had to. Fortunately, he was almost always able to win by building a strong case and explaining to the courts or the arbitrators what would happen if his approach was not followed."*
>
> **Yi Min**, *Director of Global Leadership and Organization Development, Lenovo Group, Raleigh, North Carolina, United States.*

So, from a Chinese perspective, one may argue that this vagueness in the law allows a leader to be creative in its interpretation and to use it to the advantage of the company. Compare the Lenovo story with another that I am familiar with. For obvious reasons, I cannot reveal the name of the company or the storyteller.

"My company needed to install a sign outside the building. The local government said we could not do it. I knew the government officials involved and I also knew that if I did certain things, I could get the sign approved. My boss, who was a foreigner, wanted to follow the law. As such, we did not get the sign. It would have been very easy to get around this, but the Western approach was to act according to the law. My Chinese colleagues who knew about this thought that the boss was being very foolish and did not understand how to get things done in China."

Anonymous

Some business people in China would comment that the law is meant to be broken. This is a negative way of saying what Yi Min referred to as the flexibility inherent in this vagueness that allows creative, entrepreneurial people to do just about anything that makes sense for the company, as long as others are not obviously harmed.

What both of these comments indicate is that, while the law may be intended to protect the public, it is not so rigid that it cannot be modified to meet certain needs if it can be proven that the modification is not in opposition to the public good.

Resolving Differences between the Rule of Man and the Rule of Law

While some Chinese see this issue as an opportunity for entrepreneurial thinking, this uncertainty in the legal process is a major cause of concern for many Western leaders in China. When I first arrived in China, the lack of clear legal guidelines, especially around contracts, was one of the early cultural difficulties I had as a manager. If my consulting company had a contract with another firm, I assumed that my firm would deliver certain services as spelled out in the contract, and the client company would pay the bill as agreed in the contract. Sometimes, however, the client would ask for more services than originally agreed upon but would be unwilling to pay more money for those additional services. In the beginning of my time in China, this situation made me very angry. But as I worked in the country longer, I finally realized that my idea of a contract and the client's idea were quite different. Eventually, I came up with an approach that I think can work for others.

First, make sure that both parties agree with the intent of the contract. Will it be a final document, or is it just a starting point? Two reasonable parties can move forward with either of these choices, as long as they agree in advance on the contract's intent. If it is going to be just a starting point, perhaps it should not be referred to as a "contract" but rather as a "letter of intent." If it is going to be a true contract in the Western sense, then the document should include some wording about what course either party can take if it is felt that the contract terms are not being met.

Secondly, both parties can agree that they will review progress on fulfilling the terms of the document at regular intervals. This means that you do not have to wait until the very end of the agreement period to identify differences. Chinese culture is much better at this than Western culture. Chinese people are very good at rethinking matters that may not have been considered earlier when the document was first being written. As such, they are quite flexible about modifying an agreement when it makes good business sense to do so. Westerners are often quite literal when it comes to legal documents. So, the good Chinese manager working with a Western firm or Western manager needs to be aware of this cultural difference. It is always good practice when dealing with Westerners to make this point before a problem arises.

A Few Final Tips

Leaders cannot presume right or wrong based on their own logic. Kevin Fong of the China Automobile Association (CAA) shared the following story.

> *"One day, out of the blue, four of our employees resigned. We were not warned. They just announced one day to HR that they would be leaving. They also insisted that they should be paid future compensation according to their interpretation of Chinese law. However, it is very*
>
> *(continued)*

(continued)

clear to us that, if someone voluntarily resigns, there is no legal corporate obligation to provide compensation.

I 'smelled a rat,' so I immediately contacted our regional HR head who agreed to come to China and meet with the employees. He, along with our own local HR manager, met with the four employees and taped the conversation. The employees were aware of the taping. The regional HR head asked if they would reconsider their decision and be willing to stay on. He also asked if there was a specific reason for their resignation. .

They replied that they just wanted to leave and they wanted to be paid. They were no longer interested in staying with the firm. They were then advised that, since their resignations were voluntary, there would be no additional compensation other than for the time they worked.

The four of them then took the case to arbitration. While I know that nothing is certain in the Chinese legal system, I was quite sure that we would win because we had their declaration of voluntary resignation on tape.

Much to my surprise, the arbitrators initially expressed doubt that they could rule in favor of CAA since they did not have any signed resignation letters from the employees. Furthermore, the employees' lawyer denied the authenticity of the tape, indicating that it was probably a fabrication.

Fortunately, our lawyer had lots of experience with some of these arbitrators and was able to make a convincing argument that we were indeed being truthful. We also offered to have any government agency authenticate the tape.

In this case, justice prevailed and we were not ordered to pay any additional compensation. But the lesson learned was how delicate such a matter could be. These four were clearly in the wrong, and yet they almost won because of the absence of signed letters of resignation. However, I believe that the arbitrators also understood that if they ruled in favor of the employees, they would have been setting a very dangerous precedent. All an employee would need to do to win compensation in the future would be to announce that they were through but then refuse to sign a resignation letter. No one believes that such an outcome serves justice."

Kevin Fong, *President, China Automobile Association, Beijing, China.*

So, we know that we cannot presume anything in this legal system. It is a very good practice, whether you are a Western or a Chinese leader, to have local legal guidance in each geographic area where you are located. The laws are different from location to location and, more importantly, so are the people entrusted with enforcing the laws. I AM NOT SUGGESTING THAT ONE DO ANYTHING THAT IS CORRUPT. But what I do suggest firmly is that you try to develop your *guan xi* in every location in which you have operations.

This leads to a final point about legality in China. If you have a corporate code of ethics, and nearly every Western firm has one, then everyone involved with a matter that threatens that code of ethics must understand the consequences of those ethics and the possibility of winning or losing a contract. In the two cases described above, Liu Chuanzhi of Lenovo was "flexible" with certain regulations. Lenovo is a very successful company. The other firm, described anonymously, chose to follow a Western approach. The consequence of that approach was loss of the battle.

If a leader in China believes that they, too, can be "flexible" in getting something done, but such flexibility may require actions that threaten the corporate ethical code, this action should not be taken without first obtaining corporate approval in writing. If you take action on your own, you do so at your own peril.

Notes

1   Romie F. Littrell, "Desirable Leadership Behaviors of Multi-Cultural Managers in China," *Journal of Management Development*, Vol. 21, No. 1, 2002, pp. 5–74 at p. 25.
2   W. John Hoffman and Michael J. Enright (eds.), *China into the Future* (Singapore: John Wiley & Sons (Asia), 2008), p. 55.
3   *Ibid.*, p. 99.

Chapter Thirteen Executive Summary

The Rule of Man versus the Rule of Law

- Western case law, as it applies to business, is very mature. In China, it is very immature.

- Western legal systems are based on a rule of law. The Chinese system is primarily a rule of man.

- Contracts in the West are binding documents that spell out the specifics of the terms agreed, including payment terms. Chinese contracts are often no more than "letters of intent" that provide a guideline for the future. They are typically not viewed as binding. They can be changed as conditions change or as the desires of one of the parties change.

- Contract negotiation is a sticking point for Chinese–Western negotiations. If both parties agree upfront on the nature of the contract (that is, whether it is a binding document or just a step in the negotiations), then many future problems may be avoided.

- The Western legal system presumes you are innocent until proven guilty. The Chinese system is essentially the opposite: you are presumed guilty until you can prove your innocence. This is a major dilemma for leaders whose companies are often the subjects of frivolous lawsuits from angry former employees, or from provincial officials who want something more from the relationship than currently exists.

- Chinese leaders are sometimes less rigid about the law and regulations than Westerners. Chinese will use their *guan xi* (关系) to get things done. Westerners often must depend on others (for example, local lawyers) to achieve similar results.

- Corruption and unethical behavior is not an option for a proper leader in China, but there are sometimes ways to be creative and flexible in order to achieve what is needed. In these cases, while still following a legal approach, if there is any potential danger of corporate ethics being compromised, then the leader must discuss the matter with his or her corporate legal officers as well as his or her own superiors before taking any action that could damage the company's reputation and his or her own standing in the firm.

> **"The early bird gets the worm."**
> Western proverb
>
> **"*Qiang da chu tou niao.*"**
> (枪打出头鸟,
> **"The first bird out gets shot.")**
> Chinese proverb

Chapter 14

INNOVATION AND RISK-TAKING

The Chinese are often accused of being unwilling to take risks and, therefore, of failing to be innovative. Yet, many firms in China are trying to do new things, and therefore require innovation. Mercer's Guo Xin believes that the Chinese are, in fact, innovators and risk-takers, despite their reputation for being otherwise.

"We need to realize that this is a big country with so many people. Maybe half are risk-averse and half are risk-takers. Maybe it is only 25% of the population who are risk-takers. That is still more risk-takers than there are people in America. We need to put it into perspective. Certainly there are some business settings where it is dangerous to take risks. State-owned-enterprises are an example. There is still a lot of politicizing in SOEs, so leaders there might be less willing to go out on a limb and make a mistake that could leave them open to attack by opponents or others vying for similar jobs in the Party.

In any case, I think Chinese entrepreneurs act like Western entrepreneurs. Both cultures hire lawyers to advise them against exposure. Just as it is the job of a business lawyer in the West to avoid exposure, so is it the job of a good Chinese executive."

Guo Xin, *Managing Director, Greater China, Mercer Consulting, Beijing, China.*

Guo Xin's point about the numbers of potential risk-takers in China is an important one. While the percentage of Chinese who are prepared to take business risks may be smaller than in the West, it still adds up to a huge number. Yi Min also thinks that the Chinese are more creative and innovative than they are given credit for.

> *"We are not always seen as innovative by Westerners, but I think that is because we are not always so quick to speak up. We are not brought up that way. 'The first bird out gets shot' is more useful to the Chinese than the Western proverb, 'The early bird gets the worm.' We understand the value of being first, but we see it as a secondary value to being right. Chinese people are rarely the first to speak up, but they are also rarely the last. We wait until there is enough exposure on the table before we begin to make our points.*
>
> *Sometimes, Westerners are too quick to judge and they may favor those Chinese who speak English well and early. But generally, Chinese are more deep thinking than Westerners and will do more preparation before we move. Westerners tend to be more fast-talking and fast-acting, but we see this as a leadership weakness."*
>
> **Yi Min**, *Director of Global Leadership and Organization Development, Lenovo Group, Raleigh, North Carolina, United States.*

In this case, Yi Min believes the reputation the Chinese have for not being innovative is not deserved. She believes it is related more to the Chinese preference for not speaking up loudly and quickly, as those in the West tend to do, than to their ability to be innovative.

Shi Lan of Towers Perrin describes another reason for this reputation. She talks about the Chinese concept of *tao guang yang hui* (稻光养晦, hiding your capabilities), especially in SOEs.

> *"We don't see the practice of 'tao guang yang hui' (稻光养晦) very much today in private firms. But it is still common in SOEs. The more you show of yourself, the more likelihood there can be a mistake. While the penalty for failure is not so severe in Western firms, it can spell disaster in an SOE. This concept dates back over 2,000 years, when*

(continued)

there were always political squabbles among royal families. Leaders learned to be secretive and to hide what they could do. Otherwise, an opponent could try to take advantage and improve their relative position.

Remember, the primary goal of a leader in an SOE is not necessarily to grow the firm, but rather to be promoted to a higher level."

Shi Lan, *Senior Consultant for Leadership, Towers Perrin, Beijing, China.*

In this comment, we are reminded of the main difference between SOEs and private firms, whose aim is to make a profit. Historically, Chinese firms have been state-owned, and so the practices found therein are those that are most commonly used to describe Chinese firms. But the movement toward a market economy in China has changed that.

Over the past 10 years or so, a subculture has arisen in businesses in China, especially in multinational firms. These people, mostly the younger population of workers, have become very Westernized in their thinking. They see the need for more innovation and risk-taking. Not encumbered by history, and encouraged by their Western-thinking bosses to take risks, they are less afraid of failure than their predecessors were. This is a good sign for China. But the path is still not clear. "Innovation in China was once taken to be synonymous with technical innovation. [But] increasingly (if grudgingly) China's business leaders appear to accept investments in new processes, new brands, and new management systems … but there is still a spotty record of commercially successful innovations."[1]

This comment from John Hoffman and Michael Enright supports the idea that innovation is coming to China, although they seem to believe it is not here yet.

Ren Binyan of Alcoa describes the current preference in China for getting something right over doing it first.

> *"The Chinese will still work hard on something to make sure they get it right before they introduce it to the world."*
>
> **Ren Binyan**, *Vice President, Alcoa (China), Investment Company, Ltd., Beijing, China.*

Patrick Huang is more definitive and somewhat critical of innovation in China.

> *"China is still very much a manufacturing society. Our innovativeness is more about doing something little by little. Continuous improvement, as practiced in manufacturing sites, is based on improving the process with small changes. We are not motivated to be too innovative, as so much money has been spent already on plants, equipments, and processes that are meant to be used in a defined way. Too much creativity could actually be too costly. So, until China becomes more of a service economy, like many countries in the West, it will continue to lag behind the West in innovation."*
>
> **Patrick Huang**, *Managing Director, Watson Wyatt Worldwide, Shanghai, China.*

The Chinese Bureaucracy

Any discussion of innovation and risk-taking in China, or the absence thereof, would be incomplete without mention of China's incredible bureaucracy. Here, more than anywhere else in China, a new leader will be faced with the huge barriers that arise from resistance to change. In my experience, it is highly unusual for a company in China to apply for a business permit, for example, without going through multiple application stages. Western-trained leaders are usually extremely frustrated by this process, which would not be tolerated in their own firms.

For all of the reasons described above, Chinese bureaucrats are very reluctant to say "yes" to anything without getting multiple approvals from their superiors. Unfortunately, the bureaucracy tends to be even more conventional and risk-averse when the applicant is a foreigner.

I went through the very uncomfortable experience of opening a new Watson Wyatt office in Shenzhen. The process was eventually successful, but it took a lot of effort and required much in the way of local help. After the office was operating successfully, the SARS epidemic hit and people were not permitted to travel freely in China. A year after opening, we were required to submit our annual business license renewal papers in Shenzhen, but the people who were charged with performing this chore for us worked in Shanghai, and they were unable to go to Shenzhen at the time because of the travel ban. When the ban was lifted and they went to Shenzhen to file the papers, we were penalized for lateness. The fact that it was impossible to file on time, because of a Chinese government-imposed ban, was irrelevant. In this case, we hired local lawyers and others with *guan xi*, but all to no avail. The bureaucracy would not bend. The renewal was required on a certain date and we did not meet that date. The rules were clear about late renewals. We had to pay a steep fine.

Horror stories like this are common in China and can affect everything from gaining permits and licenses, and making tax payments, to obtaining Chinese visas and various other matters.

Fortunately, most corporate employees that one will be asked to lead are not as rigid and risk-averse as the Chinese bureaucracy. Nevertheless, from time to time, every leader in China will be forced to work with them. It is wise, in that case, to get as much local assistance as possible, but also to recognize that this type of bureaucratic behavior in China will soon have to change.

What Can You Do to Improve Innovation and Risk-Taking in Your Firm?

This chapter has made the point that China is gradually becoming more innovative, but that innovation and risk-taking need to become a more significant part of the business culture. Here are a few best practices that will work in China:

- Make it clear that innovation is a requirement. Include innovation and risk-taking competencies in everyone's development plans.
- Hire people who are risk-takers. Train your human resources staff in behavioral-event interviewing techniques so that they can hire people based on the presence of risk-taking and innovativeness in their work styles. The presence of these competencies for a high-tech firm is more important than the school the candidate attended or the companies he or she has worked for.
- Reward people for being innovative. I am not talking only about paying them royalties for developing patents. Establish a program that empowers managers to grant bonuses to employees who take calculated risks, whether or not they bear fruit.
- Reassure people that they will not be penalized for making a mistake if they were trying to be innovative.
- Encourage new employees to take risks and to not feel ashamed if they make mistakes.

I have no doubt that the perceived lack of innovativeness in China will soon be a thing of the past. Fifty years ago, when Japan was rebuilding its country and starting on the road to becoming an economic superpower, the label "Made in Japan" indicated that the product was probably a cheap, poorly made copy. Today, Japan is among the leaders in innovation, from automobiles to appliances to high-tech gadgetry. I believe that the same future awaits China. Until that time comes, though, it is the job of business leaders in China to prompt their employees with the right programs and incentives to get there as quickly as possible. This will only help your company to be more successful and will guarantee your success as a leader.

In the next chapter, we will take a look at decision-making methods in China and at how a leader can help stimulate the process.

Note

1   W. John Hoffmann and Michael J. Enright (eds.), *China into the Future* (Singapore: John Wiley & Sons (Asia), 2008), p. 27.

Chapter Fourteen Executive Summary

Innovation and Risk-Taking

- The Chinese are often accused of not being risk-takers or innovators. Nevertheless, as China is quickly marching toward a place of dominance in the business world, it needs to perfect these competencies quickly and qualitatively.

- Many leaders give evidence of how the reality is changing in China. Chinese employees are slowly shedding this old label and starting to take calculated risks.

- Some Chinese believe the label is unfair, because they believe they just put more thought into innovations than do many in the West. They believe this slower approach is preferable to the Western approach, which many Chinese see as being too aggressive.

- State-owned enterprises are late in coming to the table in terms of encouraging innovativeness. There is often a fear among managers that doing something new may result in a serious mistake for which they will be punished. On the other hand, while there are remnants of this idea floating around private firms, they are much more willing to take risks and are less fearful of the consequences of failure if the risks are justifiable.

- The remaining bastion of resistance to innovativeness and risk-taking is the Chinese bureaucracy. Business leaders in China are advised not to try and tackle the bureaucracy without all kinds of help—both internal and external. This is an area that will definitely change in China, as the current practice is debilitating to businesses there. Until that happens, however, leaders need to be patient and use all the available resources to surmount the barriers that government bureaucrats will inevitably put up.

- To speed up the process of risk-taking and innovativeness in Chinese businesses, leaders are encouraged to do the following: require risk-taking as a developmental competency and make it part of everyone's development plan; hire candidates who have displayed risk-taking and innovativeness in their prior jobs; reward people for innovations; and reassure employees—and especially new employees—that they will not be penalized for making a mistake if it was done while taking a calculated risk and the potential outcome would have saved money, time, or effort.

Chapter 15

DECISION-MAKING

Western leaders are taught to seek the advice and consent of their peers and subordinates, but then to act independently and make a decision. Generally, Chinese leaders will work toward a consensus to come up with a decision that is deemed to be best for the group. Often, this kind of approach can lead to a "safe" decision—or, worse, no decision. While this would be seen as a failure in the West, in China it is often better to wait things out rather than force a decision based on one person's opinion. In this regard, Chinese employees sometimes see their Western managers as reckless and inconsiderate. On the other hand, Westerners often see the Chinese manager as indecisive. Both these situations can cause enormous frustration.

Generally, Westerners expect quick decisions and then action. The Chinese, on the other hand, do not always value the need for speed when it comes to making a decision. They tend to focus on the complexity of an issue and want to be sure that everything has been thought through before they come to a decision. This process often involves going back to the beginning and starting the thinking and discussion process over again.

Furthermore, the collectivistic worldview of the Chinese leads them to seek consensus, which often takes a long time. As was discussed in an earlier chapter, Westerners give credit to the individual who can help drive a decision and follow it through. While the Chinese approach may be a safer one in the long run, it may be met with disgruntlement by the leaders in a multinational company's home country who may be looking for quick and decisive action.

In an earlier chapter on the unique Chinese traits, we discussed holistic thinking. Decision-making in China is very much a product of this kind of thinking. Westerners prefer to arrive at conclusions by following a linear logic that separates matters into their beginning, middle, and end issues. A holistic approach has no such order. A matter may be examined in its entirety, and some aspects may be examined repeatedly. This is viewed by Westerners as illogical and inefficient.

Developing the Best Decision-Making Process in China

How can we resolve this issue happily for all? As is often the case with cultural differences, the answer lies in compromise. If the top bosses are Western and they require a quick answer, then the Chinese employees must respond accordingly. But they should not do so in a haphazard manner. One approach is to have a decision-making group available to handle just such a situation. When the Western bosses want a quick decision, the group needs to be called to order—even if it means discussing the matter by phone or email.

The group needs to select someone to be the coordinator and facilitate the meeting(s). Such a group may have its own set of rules. Instead of seeking 100 percent consensus, it may require only 75 percent, for example. If they are deadlocked at 50–50, they need to do more work quickly and then re-convene so that they can get to a clear majority.

When a decision is reached, even without 100 percent consensus, the facilitator needs to communicate the decision to the headquarters, making it clear that it is still not unanimous, and explaining where there are differences of opinion. Members of the group who originally disagreed with the decision are obligated to abide by the majority and try to make the new decision work.

This is not a perfect solution, but no compromise is ever perfect. We have a saying in English: "Don't let perfection get in the way of good work." In other words, sometimes we just need to move forward with a good plan, even though we know we do not have a perfect solution. In many of our time-based industries, this kind of quick decision-making can make the difference between being a market leader and a market follower.

Shi Lan of Towers Perrin suggests another possibility. She talks about *jue ce hui* (决策会), a special kind of meeting designed for making important decisions.

> *"Jue ce hui are not always needed. But when a group is unable to come to a conclusion on a matter, this type of meeting is valuable because it lets everyone know that the purpose is to come to a decision. There is no alternative. You may set a time limit for discussion, after which there will either be a consensus, a vote, or someone in charge will force a decision."*
>
> **Shi Lan**, *Senior Consultant for Leadership, Towers Perrin, Beijing, China.*

Patrick Huang of Watson Wyatt says that whatever method you use, eventually the leader must *pai ban* (拍板). This literally means to rap the gavel like a judge. In other words, you must eventually just decide.

> *"We Chinese are consensus builders. But if we are not getting to a decision and it is time to move on, the strong leaders will 'pai ban' (拍板). He or she will just make the final decision and that is that. It is one thing to try for consensus, but eventually, we have to stop trying and just be done with the matter. Once there is 'pai ban,' the others must follow. If not, it is a sign of weakness in the leader."*
>
> **Patrick Huang**, *Managing Consultant, Watson Wyatt Worldwide, Shanghai, China.*

Leaders in China must understand the value of both the Western and Chinese approaches to decision-making. When there is a problem between these different approaches, the leader needs to get an agreement upfront from all the parties on the process that will be followed. As a rule of thumb in China, I recommend using the Chinese approach. If necessary, you can also incorporate methods of finalizing a decision, such as holding a decision-making meeting (决策会, *jue ce hui*) and having everyone understand that the leader can *pai ban* (拍板) if necessary.

As is often the case, higher-ups in the headquarters may require a decision by a specific time. In this case, the local leader needs to explain that contingency to the others on the team from which he or she hopes to gain consensus. In this way, everyone understands that they are time-limited and that their goal is to come to a decision.

No company can afford to be frozen. Doing so spells disaster. The Chinese holistic and collectivist approach to decision-making certainly has its merits. But the Western approach of getting to a decision point is also valuable in the current competitive business market. It may have been acceptable in the days of government-sponsored state-owned enterprises not to force decisions in a timely fashion, but it is no longer true today. Leaders in China need to bridge this gap.

Chapter Fifteen Executive Summary

Decision-Making

- Westerners believe in the value of making quick decisions and then taking action. The Chinese want to be sure that all angles of an issue are reviewed first, and all matters are thought through, before coming to a conclusion. This process often involves going back to the beginning and restarting the thinking and the discussion process. These two different approaches may be sources of frustration for both parties.

- The collectivistic culture of the Chinese leads to a consensus-building, decision-making approach. Westerners view this approach as slow and inefficient. The Western individualistic style, on the other hand, leads to an approach where the leader sees the need to drive a decision and force it to be followed through. The Chinese often see this method as being overly aggressive and possibly dangerous.

- The Chinese are typically holistic thinkers. This allows them to view an issue at once in all of its complexity. The Westerner, who is typically more of a linear thinker, prefers to tackle a problem in a certain order. This involves a beginning, a middle, and an end. If this order is violated, the Westerner sees a flawed process. The Chinese, on the other hand, see the Western approach as too rigorous and inflexible.

- In China, it is best for a leader initially to embrace the Chinese approach, since it is the one that the majority of the team members will be most comfortable with. In that regard, the leader also needs to use one or more methods such as *jue ce hui* (决策会) and *pai ban* (拍板) to force decisions if required.

- Leaders in China cannot afford to let too much time go by before taking a decision, as this will lead to a loss of competitive advantage. On the other hand, the leader needs to be assured that the others in the firm buy into the decision and will effectively carry it out. This is why the leadership challenge is to bridge these two approaches. They both have much value, but they also have their downsides.

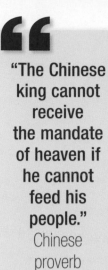

Chapter 16

INFLUENCING EMPLOYEE MOTIVATION

This may be a good time to go back and reread the first few paragraphs of the preface to this book, where I described the MBA course I was teaching. One of the employees asked me whether Western motivational techniques could actually work in China because, in his experience, employees did not expect their managers to help them with motivation. As noted, this led to my deeper understanding of how some of the most basic Western leadership practices could be a poor fit in China. A leader trying to help develop employee motivation is a prime example of this dichotomy.

Yet, when I speak with new managers, one of the most common questions I hear is, "How can I keep employees motivated?" Managers tell me that a newly hired employee is often very self-motivated and hardworking. But after one or two years, productivity drops and the employee no longer seems as motivated as at the time of hire.

This is a normal reaction for someone who finds his or her work repetitive and has become unsure about what to do next. When they are first hired, they are very excited to have the job and to prove themselves as good workers. But after a time, employees are no longer worried about needing to prove something. Rather, they become very internally-focused and begin to think about whatever is most important to them. So, what does a good leader do in this case, especially in China, where jobs for talented workers are so bountiful and you do not want to lose your best people?

Can Anyone "Motivate" Anyone Else?

We often hear people talk about "motivating" employees. But can you really do this? Motivation is an internal drive that makes us do what we do. As the Americans say: "You can lead a horse to water, but you cannot make it drink."

In my view, a leader does not provide the initial motivation. That comes from within the employee. It is already there and is based on a combination of genetics and character traits that were formed in their early developmental years. But what a good leader can do is first acknowledge that different employees have different psychological makeups and are therefore motivated differently. Secondly, he or she must recognize that different types of employee groups (men versus women, highly educated versus non-educated, professional versus blue-collar, and so on) are also motivated differently. Finally, the very good leader will be able to identify his or her employees' different motivations and try to influence them in the workplace.

For most of us, we do our best work when we take a project personally. It is when we believe we can do something valuable— either for our companies, our clients, our colleagues, or ourselves— that we perform our best work. In other words, motivation is internal and personal. When we say there is something external about motivation, what we really mean is that there are certain factors outside of us that can influence our internal needs and desires. It is the manager's job to discover and use these external factors for each employee under his or her supervision.

Many new leaders in China do not realize that they are among the strongest external motivators that exist at work. In fact, even if you don't try to influence your employees, this has a significant effect on employees. However, that influence is negative. It is often "demotivational," because the employees think that the managers do not care about them. Leaders in China should always be aware of this influence on employees, especially their youngest and newest employees. These employees are most in need of direction and influence. One of the key reasons that people leave a firm prematurely is that they believe their managers do not care enough about them to help them succeed. This is true not only in China, but everywhere there are businesses designed to make a profit. Good leaders regularly ask themselves: "Am I positively or negatively influencing my employees' motivation?"

Westerners believe that the first job of a leader is to keep his or her employees motivated. Leaders should be able to articulate a clear vision about where the company is going, how it is going to get there, and what the employees need to do to help it do so. We find managers in Western firms in China attempting to emulate this style. But in Chinese firms, especially those that are still more-or-less state-owned, we find many leaders more interested in looking upward at the Communist Party rather than downward at the employees. These Chinese leaders understand that the Party has a much greater influence on their future than the success of their workforce. Thus, their focus on employees is more complicated than just motivating them. Rather, they are interested in getting them to have the right political attitude.

Patrick Huang shares a story about this.

"In China, we have a one-child policy. These days, however, many women get around this by having a second child and paying a 'fine' to the government that permits their second child the same benefits enjoyed by first children. If you are unemployed or work for a private company, it is okay to do this. But if you are a manager in a state-owned enterprise, and one of your employees has a second child, you will be fired. This is officially not permitted under the one-child policy. So, what most SOE managers do is fire the employee before the baby is born. Otherwise, the manager will lose his or her job."

Patrick Huang, *Managing Director, Watson Wyatt Worldwide, Shanghai, China.*

In a private firm, when a woman becomes pregnant with a second child, this is a source of excitement and congratulations from most employees. In a Chinese state-owned firm, the pregnant employee will most likely be fired.

Now let us take a look at an example of mismatched motivation in China.

> *"Employees at one of our plants were instructed in the safety concerns of riding bicycles. Safety is a core value at Alcoa. All leaders take this very seriously. In this case, the leader was a Westerner. He put lots of effort into ensuring that employees wore helmets when riding their bicycles, even at home. Also, there were posted speed limits that everyone needed to adhere to when riding their bikes. Riding slowly and not running were important issues. But to the employees, these precautions were unnecessary and primarily served to slow down operations, thus reducing their chances to earn a large production-based bonus. The Westerner says: 'No running.' The employee says: 'It's not risky. Just let me be.'*
>
> *Another safety regulation is that you are not permitted to use a cell phone while walking. Employees see this as too intrusive. The leader believes he is providing a safe work environment, which should be motivational. The employee sees it as too restrictive and demotivational."*
>
> **Janet Zhong**, *Vice President, Human Resources, Asia Pacific, Alcoa (China) Investment Company, Ltd., Beijing, China.*

In this case, the leader wants to provide a safe environment for the employees. But the employees weigh that against the time it will take to get the job done, which can affect their bonus. This kind of mismatch happens all around the world. But it is particularly common in China when the leader and the followers have different needs.

Yi Min offers another comment on managing and influencing employee motivation in China.

> *"Westerners tend to manage with an open and personable approach that implies sincere caring and respect for people. Some Chinese leaders find it difficult to do this. Many of them were not brought up to*

(continued)

be so open and to praise people in public. From the perspective of the employees, they may not be used to this type of behavior that Westerners tend to display when working with them. It is important for Westerners to understand this and be careful that their best intentions are not perceived with suspicion by employees."

Yi Min, Director of Global Leadership and Organization Development, Lenovo Group, Raleigh, North Carolina, United States.

Yi Min's example underscores the second theme of this book, which is that it is naïve to think that you can simply import best Western practices on leadership to China and expect that they will work as well as they do in the West.

In the traditional Chinese business culture, rather than rewarding employees with motivational incentives, the focus was on not making mistakes and punishing people when they did. There is a famous case study about Haier Corporation, the China-based multinational appliance manufacturer when it ventured into its first US operation. In China, when Haier employees made mistakes, they were publicly punished and sometimes humiliated. When Haier applied this approach in America, there was outright revolt. A strike was threatened until Haier reneged on this practice and tried instead to follow a more Western approach.

"Chinese leaders are good at finding mistakes. This is one way that they show capability as a subject matter expert. This is basically a punishment culture. We find mistakes and then punish employees for them. Some call it 'management by fear.' Liu Chuanzhi, the founder of Lenovo, used military discipline when he first started. He had a rule about coming late to a meeting. If someone was late, he or she was punished by having to stand for a minute before sitting down and joining the meeting."

Yi Min, Director of Global Leadership and Organization Development, Lenovo Group, Raleigh, North Carolina, United States.

According to most psychological theories, punishment is the opposite of rewarding. You can never motivate through punishment. Rather, you can instill fear, which may prevent someone from behaving in a particularly undesirable way. But this is not motivational; it is just caution. Punishment does not breed risk-taking and innovativeness. Rather, it promotes conventional thinking and avoidance.

Jim Leininger of Watson Wyatt believes that it is very motivational for Chinese employees to have leaders whom they see as strong and decisive.

> *"Chinese employees want their leaders to be very capable, strong, and decisive. They are also expected to be parent-like and show their caring with real results. Finding a job for a spouse or helping with the care of an employee's sick parent are examples of what leaders can do to motivate employees in China."*
>
> **Jim Leininger**, *General Manager, Watson Wyatt Worldwide, Beijing, China.*

How to Influence Chinese Employee Motivation

This may be seen as counter-intuitive to a culture with a high power-distance, but that is all the more reason why such humanistic behavior is so valued when it comes from a leader.

The Challenge for Westerners. For Westerners who are new leaders in China, it is possible that many of their preconceptions about raising employees' performance to the highest levels, helping them to develop their careers and become better leaders, will simply fall on deaf ears. Some employees may consider them too "Western" in their thinking and totally misguided. Westerners, on the other hand, may see these employees as feeling threatened and unwilling to try new approaches.

Li Jianbo believes that Western leaders can win over employees by paying close attention to them and not just following policies and guidelines.

> *"Westerners are very good at following set policies and procedures. The Chinese managers, on the other hand, have fewer policies and procedures to go by. Therefore, they tend to think first about the employees, rather than the procedures. This is usually inefficient. But it works in China. Rather than follow formal procedures, Chinese leaders will build informal channels through informal means, such as eating and drinking with their immediate subordinates. At these informal meetings, most matters get worked out. Employees feel a connection with the leaders and are motivated to perform well for them. This kind of personal commitment is more motivational for Chinese employees than the formal Western approach of following prescribed policies and procedures."*
>
> **Li Jianbo**, *Vice President, Human Resources, Cisco Systems (China), Beijing, China.*

So, the question of how to influence motivation remains. How does an "enlightened" leader in China truly help employees to be motivated? How does one avoid being seen as only being there to squeeze more out of the employees, rather than helping them to do better so that they enjoy their work more?

There is at least a two-part answer to this question. First, you need to truly believe that motivated employees will be better producers than non-motivated employees, and will be more likely to stay engaged with the company than to leave for another offer. If you do believe this, then your own behavior needs to show this in all of your contacts with your employees. The manager who believes these things is interested in the employee as a person, not just as a worker. Everyone is very busy, but it is the manager's first job to be there for his or her employees and to understand what motivates them.

Secondly, you need to have patience. These best Western practice motivational techniques are still new to China and require time to be universally accepted. In the meantime, work gradually on this and do not expect too much progress to occur overnight.

Now let us look at a few examples of what might motivate different employees. Does the employee love the company and really want to see the firm succeed? Does the employee care more about his or her own career, rather than the firm? Or, is the employee focused more on his or her family, or on some other aspect of his or her personal life? No matter what the primary motivation, the employee can still be more productive if the manager understands these personal motivations and tries to arrange assignments that are geared directly to each employee.

For example, in the case of the employee who loves the firm, it is easy to give him or her assignments that are clearly important to the firm's success and to let the employee know that his or her success is directly connected to the company's success. To the second employee, who is more concerned about his or her own career than about the firm, the manager must point out the significance of this particular experience to the employee's advancement and how it will help his or her career—either at the same firm or elsewhere in the market. For the third employee, who is more focused on his or her personal life, the manager can try to arrange assignments that allow the employee more time to himself or herself. Of course, in this case, the manager needs to explain that this approach will most likely impede the employee's promotion in the firm, but it is still important to keep the person motivated so that he or she is making these allowances. (Many firms will not allow this luxury, and such an employee will always feel frustrated there.)

The point is that we are all motivated for different reasons, and it is the manager's job to identify those reasons and try to influence them. In China, we must be mindful of the employee's initial suspicions. But if you keep your promises and are open about your intentions, over time, this approach will sink in and you can overcome the employee's doubts.

Finally, when considering employee motivation in China, never forget about "face."

> *"We had a Chinese employee who declared to his Western boss that he wanted to be a plant manager some day. The boss was surprised by this and said honestly: 'Well, I did not have a plan for you to be a plant manager, but I will think about it and get back to you.'*

(continued)

After some consideration, the boss decided it was a good idea to make this man a plant manager and got back to the employee with the news. But it was already too late. His previous comment had already caused the employee to lose face. He declined the boss's offer and left the firm."

Janet Zhong, *Vice President, Human Resources, Asia Pacific, Alcoa (China) Investment Company, Ltd., Beijing, China.*

In the next chapter, we continue to discuss the theme of motivation, but with a focus on the team, rather than the individual.

Chapter Sixteen Executive Summary

Influencing Employee Motivation

- Keeping employees motivated is a challenge for any leader in any country. In China, there are some special considerations.

- Chinese employees are sometimes suspicious of their leaders when they try to influence motivation. While it is common in the West to do this, in China it is sometimes seen as just another trick to increase production.

- Some Chinese leaders in state-owned enterprises are more concerned with their status in the Communist Party than with the motivation of their employees. Therefore, employees who have an SOE background are sometimes skeptical about their leaders' attempts to provide incentives to motivate them.

- In China's short business history, using military-style discipline and handing out punishments for mistakes, and thus instilling a fear of humiliation, has been a typical approach for keeping people motivated. The rewarding style of Western management is therefore somewhat alien to the Chinese way of thinking in business. While the "management by fear" approach is rarely seen in multinational companies in China today, it is still not that old and occasionally influences the management techniques of some Chinese business leaders.

- To successfully influence motivation in Chinese employees, a leader should worry less about policies and procedures, and focus more on the specific needs of the individual. This will gain you respect and will more often lead to improved employee motivation than will a focus on sticking to the words in the policies and procedures manual.

- Leaders should recognize the diverse needs of different employees and attempt to have separate motivational plans for them based on those different needs.

Chapter 17

TEAMWORK

In the previous chapter, we looked at influencing the motivation of employees who make up business teams in China. In this chapter, we will look at the team itself. There is both good news and bad news to report about teams in China. Watson Wyatt's *Work China* research conducted in 2003 produced a very interesting finding in regards to teamwork. The study looked at over 10,000 employees in China. They mostly worked for multinational firms, although a small sample of local Chinese firms was also included. The study found that Chinese business teams were essentially stronger than business teams in the West, especially as compared to the US norm. But when they looked at cross-functional team cooperation, they found a much weaker relationship than is typically found in the West.[2]

My interpretation of this finding is that teams are strong internally in China because they are representative of a family. As we already know about the strength of the Chinese family, there is strong loyalty and interdependence. This, I believe, has been transferred in the workplace to the team to which an employee belongs. But just like elsewhere in China, loyalty lessens and hostility increases as you leave the main hub: the family. So, the kind of competition and mistrust that may exist between families in China may also exist between business teams.

As an executive coach, I have heard this in nearly every company I have worked with in China. It does not matter if it is a local firm or a multinational. As long as the employees are primarily Chinese, this phenomenon of strong internal teams but weak cross-functional cooperation is very common.

So, the issue for the leader is not to attempt to strengthen teamwork. It is already as strong as anywhere else in the world. The challenge is to improve the cross-team collaboration that is so necessary if a company is to run smoothly.

Dealing with Weak Cross-Functional Teamwork in China

There are many training groups in China that try to help solve this dilemma with team-building exercises. One such firm, interestingly named I Will Not Complain, is an Asian strategy development firm which began as a training firm that organized team-building exercises at the Great Wall outside of Beijing. Their approach has worked well and has demonstrated some noteworthy improvements.

Leigh Baker, an Australian strategy consultant in Beijing, has been using the Myers-Briggs Type Indicator® (MBTI) to test the compatibility of diverse team members based on their particular personality types. The idea is that if you know the ways in which you—and others in the firm with whom you must interact—make judgments and develop perceptions, you will have a better chance of working well together.

Christopher Earley and Soon Ang, in their book *Cultural Intelligence*,[3] have developed a method of measuring cultural intelligence (CQ). By measuring the CQs of various team members, one can gain a better sense of the cultural differences between them. The reason for doing this, as stated earlier, is that people of different ages and from different towns may have very different cultural profiles from others who are from the same national culture. Their CQ gives a more precise indicator of the way they psychologically process cultural information and, therefore, of the way they relate to others with different CQs.

Hala Helmy of Mundipharma describes a less scientific way of strengthening her team in Beijing.

"A leader must listen very carefully because there is often passive resistance. We can do it here. I can ask and get an answer. I set directives and make them very clear. I try to share as much as possible with the senior team. We meet formally every week. In the beginning, they were in silos. No collaboration. Now they tend to move in the same direction. I inform and include and enable. We often need to have very long discussions and I must be culturally sensitive.

Having said that, however, I must admit that, as a foreigner, you don't ever get it completely. You think you've got it, and then something happens and you realize you don't.

But the team has become stronger over time. We are all very open with each other and we seem to have broken down the silos and are working together to get the best results. But it is a never-ending process."

Hala Helmy, President, Mundipharma, Beijing, China.

In my executive coaching experience, I have often recommended job rotation. Moving team members, including team leaders, to other teams will help break down some of the barriers that are formed over time. The rotated team members now have new learning curves, but in the long run, this approach will help cross-team collaboration. I suggest doing this in a planned way. Simply hearing the leader explain that the process will help teams work better together has a positive impact. It also helps job enrichment, as people will not get stuck in a rut as might occur if they stayed on the same team. If the teams are essentially serving the same function, I also recommend changing team leaders every six to 12 months.

In China, work competition between teams is common. Using this as an external exercise, through sports or games, may also be beneficial as a way to get to know other team members. However, I suggest minimizing this approach within the workplace, as it could lead to some teams hoping for the failure of other teams in their work process. In a worst-case scenario, one team may actually sabotage another team's efforts. (I have seen this happen!) This is a disastrous outcome and not one that any leader would want to provoke. As such, I recommend the alternative approach, which is to reward multi-team progress. This can be done using an incentive plan, or a special bonus plan, or it may even be in the form of public celebrations of multi-team successes.

Until Chinese internal teams work better together than they do currently, China will be at a disadvantage compared to other countries. It is up to the leaders to bring about this improvement.

Perhaps the leaders can initiate improvements in this area through external coaching, the subject of a later chapter. But now we turn to one of the "touchier" subjects in Chinese business: leading the process of reward management.

Notes

1   James M. Kouzes and Barry Y. Posner, *The Leadership Challenge*, 3rd edition (San Francisco: Jossey-Bass, 2002), p. 241.
2   Watson Wyatt Worldwide, *Work China* (Beijing: 2003).
3   P. Christopher Earley and Soon Ang, *Cultural Intelligence* (Stanford, CA: Stanford University Press, 2003).

Chapter Seventeen Executive Summary

Teamwork

- Chinese teams are very strong. Team members are loyal to the team and committed to its success. There is a clear analogy with the Chinese family, the foundation of Chinese society.

- Despite the strength of these teams, however, there is very little cross-team collaboration, as in the West, and which is now so necessary in China.

- There are many programs in China to help improve cross-team collaboration. These include team-building exercises, and psychological and/or cultural tests of team members aimed at understanding their individual motivations as well as those of the members of other teams with whom they must work more effectively.

- Job rotation across teams is another recommended approach to narrow the gap between teams.

- Competition between teams through sports or games can be a good bridge between different teams. However, it is best to minimize inter-team competition at work, as this can lead to efforts to sabotage the potential success of the other teams.

Chapter 18

REWARDING EXECUTIVES IN CHINA

This now famous quote attributed to Deng Xiaoping is anathema to the China of the 1950s and 1960s, when communism first swept through China and "capitalist roadsters" were persecuted and killed, or were forced to flee the country. Today, the Chinese are tripping over one another in their quest to make money. While the real entrepreneurial spirit in China is found in the countless small businesses that manufacture everything from antibiotics to zippers, there are many workers who are looking to get rich from their companies through salaries and perquisites. This poses a challenge to business leaders in China, where inflation, though now on the rise, is still lower than the typical salary movement. For example, between 2007 and 2009, the reported annual inflation rate in China ranged from 3 percent to 5 percent, while estimated salary growth was between 7 percent and 9 percent. If it were not for the economic crisis, the salary increase rates would have been higher. The forecasted average salary increase rate for China for 2010 is 9 percent. In some economically booming locations (such as Suzhou, outside of Shanghai), and with jobs that are in high demand (such as computer engineers), salary increases have averaged over 12 percent. How can companies keep up with this? They cannot charge proportionately more for their products or services, but must pay more for their staff.

The situation is further complicated by the fact that salaries in China are not always doled out in a strategic way. Rather, they are often used as a means to hire or retain someone, regardless of what the market says the job is worth. This process, in turn, distorts the salary market and artificially raises pay to levels well above the value the job can provide for the company. While this pattern has been seen before (during the high-tech bubble in the US in the 1990s, for example), it is one of the most difficult to manage. If you come to China today, this is exactly what you will face.

Finally, there is the socio-cultural issue of what salary means to the average Chinese worker. It is not only a means for paying one's bills. A high salary is also a badge of honor, with one's family and friends well aware of the amount one receives. It is as common for co-workers to openly discuss their pay amounts as it is for them to discuss how much they pay for rent and for their new watches. Business leaders in China need to be aware of this before awarding salary increases or making salary adjustments within their firms. While one can "mandate" that the amount of everyone's salary should be kept confidential, one should not expect that this will be followed.

> *"What everyone needs to understand about pay in China is that many employees belong to the first generation in their families who do not have to struggle to find food or shelter that they can afford. When I was a child, I had relatives in the countryside who were often forced to eat leaves that they could find in the woods and suck on them for any kind of nourishment. Employees who remember those days, or at least have heard about them, are pretty serious about making enough money to assure their parents and other relatives that what they make is more than enough for them to live on."*
>
> **Kevin Fong**, *President, China Automobile Association, Beijing, China.*

I learned the hard way about the nuances of pay in China. Soon after arriving in the country, I made a strategic salary adjustment for one of the key employees in my firm. I was used to doing this often in the US, and I believed I was doing it for the right reasons. I discussed it with the employee and his manager, and the employee was thrilled. I went home that night feeling it was money well invested. Much to my dismay, within a few days, there was grumbling in the office. After lots of questioning about what was going on, I learned that the news was out about the salary adjustment and the other employees were planning to line up for adjustments to their salaries as well. This was several years ago, when the concept of "pay for performance" was not regularly practiced in China. I was able to resolve the situation by having individual salary discussions with all of the disgruntled employees and making adjustments where I thought they were warranted. In most cases, we were able to identify what performance changes would be required in order to receive more pay. But, in retrospect, I wish I had known this would happen *before* I had to go through it all, rather than after the fact. I believe I would not have been so cavalier about making the original salary adjustment had I known better.

Most multinational firms have been using rewards strategically for many years in their home countries. However, one of the more difficult concepts to grasp for companies in China, both multinational and domestic, is *how* to reward employees. That is, companies easily figure out how much to pay. They just don't do it strategically. Not too long ago in China, pay and benefits management was merely a distribution program. The only management decisions were logistical ones. When should we pay? How do we process benefit claims? Central or provincial or local governments set salary and benefit levels, and there was little or no discretion for managers. The idea that high-performing employees would be paid differently from average performers was alien to nearly all Chinese businesses. Concepts such as market-based pay, performance-based pay, and incentive pay, while commonplace everywhere else in the world, were not even discussed in China.

Let us break down the China reward management discussion into three parts: base compensation (including non-monetary rewards), incentive pay, and executive pay. Certainly, the techniques for each of these are different; but, more importantly for this discussion, so are the strategies for using them.

Base Compensation

Most companies in China have only recently begun to understand that rewards can be a strategic weapon that can give a company a strategic advantage over a competitor. In many cases, however, companies in China still see rewards in the old way. They tend to pay people based on their titles or longevity, even if their performance does not warrant what they receive. Furthermore, it is quite unusual for companies to use pay and benefits to help drive (or even reinforce) their strategic objectives. Until Chinese firms learn how to do this well, they will continue to be at a competitive disadvantage compared to those firms that use their reward programs strategically.

> *"Pay in China is still not very well understood. We are only now looking at data to see what a job is worth in the market. Before this scientific approach, we used to pay what we thought we needed to pay in order to get the employee. We were also very concerned with equity with other employees. Now, we base our pay entirely on performance, but this is a relatively new concept in China and still one that often gets questioned by employees here."*
>
> **Gao Yong**, *President, Career International, Inc., Beijing, China.*

Another issue that is common all around the world (not just in China) is the exclusion of non-monetary rewards from the consideration of what is important in a reward program. The term "total rewards" refers to all forms of reward, both monetary and non-monetary. This is very important today, as companies worry about getting the most return on their investment in rewards. Non-monetary rewards do not cost very much compared to monetary ones, and yet their impact on employees is often greater than that of monetary rewards. When thinking of "total" rewards, we need to quickly get beyond the idea of money. Total rewards include anything that provides a reward for the employee for being an associate of the company. Of course, it includes pay and benefits, but it also includes non-cash recognition, career development, training, special projects and assignments, and other items in the work environment that are intended to be rewarding.

This is not to imply that non-monetary rewards can take the place of pay in China. For the aforementioned reasons, this is certainly not the case. But if your pay is competitive, what can move you ahead of your competition is a good non-monetary reward program.

I had an experience when I was at Watson Wyatt that proved this point to me very soundly. Our office in Beijing had two employees who were there for a specific project, on loan from another Watson Wyatt office. They were with us for about six months. When it was their time to return home, I honored them both with framed certificates that recognized their dedication and hard work during their time in the Beijing office. About six months later, I ran into one of the employees. He told me that he had hung the certificate on the wall in his home office and that he appreciated it more than a bonus. He said that he would have spent a bonus and then forgotten about it. But the certificate reminded him every day of the project and the great time he had working in Beijing. This certificate cost us just a few yuan, but the retention value and goodwill it provided the firm was priceless.

In the nine years that I have lived in China, the corporate view on reward management has changed dramatically. Companies are thinking more strategically and have begun looking at the total rewards package. However, there is still a long way to go. Many companies, especially domestic companies, are still behaving as they did before China moved from a planned economy to a market economy. The longer a company waits to reward strategically, the longer it will continue to lose business and talent to its competitors.

Incentives

Many people believe that they can borrow the design of an incentive compensation program from somewhere else and simply apply it to their company in China. For instance, as a consultant, I've had an employer ask me to install the same plan they had heard we installed at a competitor.

This approach will almost invariably fail. An incentive plan must be tailored to your company's specific needs, because it is designed to help your employees behave in certain ways and achieve specific goals. Some other company's plan, or the plan you used in your home country, may not have any relevance to your China goals and your own culture. As such, borrowing another company's great plan is like borrowing a friend's great dress. Most of us are not built the same way. While the dress may look stunning on your friend, it does not mean it will automatically look stunning on you.

Incentive plans are now quite common in China, especially in multinational firms. Generally, Chinese employees like the concept because good plans provide clear goals and objectives. Employees know just what they need to do to be rewarded.

To design your own tailored plan, you need answers to several basic questions. These questions are related to your corporate goals, your China-specific goals, and your specific work culture.

There are at least four major issues that every incentive plan must address. Within these major issues are several sub-questions. Many of the answers to these questions already exist in the human resources department. Others will need to be discussed with other executives. In any case, you must obtain the answers before you can move on with the design.

The major issues are: (1) Who will participate in the plan? (2) What are the incentive plan performance measures? (3) What will be the payout formula? (4) How will you administer the plan?

Participation.   Who is eligible to participate in the plan? Will it be by organization level, geography, business unit, or some other selection criterion? What about part-time or contract employees? What about people who changed their jobs or their locations during the year? Will you pro-rate their participation if the new job has a different participation status than the former job? What about new employees? Some companies require a certain amount of time in the job to be eligible to participate. They feel that newer employees have not had enough time to impact the goals. A minimum of six months' employment is common.

Will there be a minimum performance level for employees? Some firms require a certain score on an employee's performance evaluation in order to participate in an incentive plan.

Do not confuse eligibility with participation. Based on some of your answers to the above questions, an employee may become eligible for participation, but because of poor performance, early termination, or some other factor, they may not participate in the plan.

Performance Measures. Designing performance measures is a very individual exercise and should be the job of the company, not a consultant. In my experience in China, many firms ask the consultant to design these measures based on key performance indicators (KPIs) that exist in the market. But if you do that, you are not tailoring your plan to your own company. Your plan becomes a copy of some other company's plan. It is useful to ask the consultant to offer suggestions on KPIs or other forms of performance measures that are used by companies in your industry. But the final job is the leader's, not the consultant's.

Before selecting the specific measures, it is a good idea to think about whether they should be corporate-wide, business unit- or function-specific, or individually-based. Many incentive plans use all three criteria, while some specify only one or two. The choice really depends on the firm and its intention for the plan. Is the plan designed to help the company improve one of its existing corporate measures (say, revenue or profit), or to help a business unit improve its market share, or to help individuals be better performers? The answer to this question will make it much easier to select appropriate measures.

It is quite common for a company to have multiple measures—perhaps some corporate, some business unit or function, and some individual. This brings up the subject of the *weight* of the measure. This is the relative value of one measure compared to another in any individual's incentive plan. These weights are usually varied, depending on the participant's organization level. Senior executives typically have a high weight on corporate and business unit measures in their own plans, while junior staff members typically have individual measures as the most highly weighted. For example, a China CEO's measures may be based 100 percent on China performance. A China business unit leader's incentive may be based 30 percent on China performance, 60 percent on business unit, and 10 percent on individual measures. An individual contributor's incentive plan may be based 50 percent on functional measures and 50 percent on individual measures.

Having sub-weights in each category may further complicate this process. In other words, 50 percent of your measures may be based on individual objectives. But there may be five individual objectives, each with a weight of 10 percent. The way a company determines these measures and their respective weights is reflective of its culture and unique goals. This is why it rarely works to borrow performance measures from another firm. In China, since these kinds of measures are still so new, my advice is to begin with a very simple plan and limit the number of measures to as few as will make sense strategically. You can always modify the plan later.

Measures can be financial, operational, customer-focused, or developmental (for individuals). When you use non-financial measures, it is difficult to calculate gain, so the determination of how much improvement is necessary becomes a subjective task of the manager. A common approach is to make the goal a stretch over the prior year, but not so great a stretch as to be deemed unobtainable.

Payout Formula.   This is the heart of the incentive plan and is often the most difficult to explain to employees, especially those who have not participated in such a plan before, as is often the case in China. The rule of thumb is to use as simple a formula as possible, but often that is more easily said than done, especially when there are multiple intentions for the plan and/or there are many different stakeholders. Here are a few fundamentals.

The term "target" is used in incentive plan design. It refers both to the expected achievement (target goal) and the payout for that achievement (target payout). As noted earlier, when you are looking at a financial measure, you can calculate gain from achieving the target goal. In that case, you can determine how much of that gain should be shared with employees at different levels. But when you use non-financial measures, you cannot easily calculate gain, so the target payout must be a best guess on the part of the designers. Typically, this decision is made by a group that includes the finance department as well as the line managers.

Target payouts typically vary depending on the employee level. More senior employees tend to have higher incentive targets than junior employees. This is because it is assumed that higher-level employee performance has a greater impact on corporate performance than that of junior-level employees. In China, the target payouts are a bit lower on a percentage basis than what is found in the West. As a rule of thumb for China, a senior employee may have an incentive target payout of about 30 percent of base salary, while a mid-level employee's target payout would be between 15 and 20 percent, and a very junior employee's at 5 percent.

Alternatively, a company may decide that everyone in the firm potentially makes an equal contribution. In that case, it may decide to make everyone's target the same in terms of either the percentage of base salary (for example, everyone gets a 20 percent incentive target) or the amount of renminbi (for example, everyone gets RMB20,000). While this is very egalitarian, my experience is that it is not well received in China. Employees in China generally prefer to be paid according to their actual worth, and they know that everyone is not worth the same.

Another alternative, related to the above, is to use a team-based incentive. In this case, you set team performance goals and then reward the team members based on their contribution. This can be just one part of an incentive plan or the gist of the entire plan. This approach is appreciated because it reinforces team solidarity.

Another consideration when devising a payout formula is whether there needs to be a threshold at which payouts commence. Some firms introduce these thresholds (also called "triggers" or "gates") to ensure that a certain minimum performance is reached prior to any payout. Alternatively, a firm may modify its incentive payments downward if, for example, only 50 percent, or only 80 percent, of the target performance is attained. These decisions are based on how much of a stretch is involved in the target performance measure and/or how important it is to give some incentive during that particular year. For example, a company may be fearful of losing people to the competition, so they want to give at least some incentive payment that year. In that case, partial payouts may be granted for less-than-target performance.

On a more positive note, the company should address how to handle above-target performance payouts. Should they be granted at all? If yes, should there be a gradual and continuous increase in payout as the performance exceeds target, or should it be in discrete steps? The latter is easier to administer but is not directly correlated with performance. Also, with the step approach, participants (especially in sales) might try to shift their performance to the next time period if an increased performance in the current period will not mean any new incentive payout because it is not sufficient to reach the next step. Another consideration when looking at payouts for above-target performance is whether to *cap* the payouts. This means that there will be a maximum payout, no matter what the performance level. This feature is most often used in sales when a company does not want to give a one-time "windfall" payment to someone who got very lucky during that period. It is also used when there are multiple measures and you do not want employees to concentrate just on one measure at the expense of the others.

Finally, you will need to consider how you express the target and describe it to your employees. Targets may be identified as a flat renminbi amount, as a percentage of base salary, or as a percentage of the median of the employee's pay grade. These executives should consider not only the financial implications of the choice, but also which choice best fits with the company culture. Again, this decision is usually made by the leader with the help of a group of executives, including those from finance and human resources.

In addition to determining the target payouts, the payout formula needs to account for whether the payouts will be paid in cash or non-cash (time, other goods, and so on). You also must determine if you will pay out annually, quarterly, or at some other regular interval, or on the achievement of a particular outcome.

As noted earlier, the payout formula is the heart of the incentive plan design. It takes into account many factors and can be very complicated to communicate.

Administration of the Plan. While administrative matters are often left out of the plan design and thinking, they are a vital part of the plan, especially in China where these plans have been in use for such a short period. Some of the more common issues are: the effective dates of the plan, pro-ration, handling transfers and/or resignations, the timing of payouts, the responsible department for answering employee questions, and how disputes will be handled. Addressing these matters up front, and determining how they will be handled in the compensation plan, is required for transparency, which is an important issue in China today.

Executive Pay

Executives are different from other employees. If they are doing their jobs well, their impact will be felt in the company, not only over the current year but over the long term as well. Most sophisticated companies believe that this impact should be rewarded. In other words, in addition to a base salary and an annual incentive plan, executives should also receive compensation for their long-term impact. This compensation can be paid either in cash or in stock. The stock issue in China is still complicated and requires legal and/or compensation consulting advice. Certainly, if a company wants to provide stock to executives, either in the form of grants or options, they would be wise to seek legal counsel to be sure that their plan will meet the scrutiny of Chinese and provincial laws. This is especially true for multinational firms if their Chinese employees are expected to own foreign company shares.

Rather than focus on the technicalities of Chinese law and accounting regulations, which I do not claim to have any expertise in, I will instead look at the strategic decisions a firm must make when considering executive rewards.

Reasons for Providing Executive Compensation in China. The first decision a company needs to make when thinking about rewarding its executives differently from the rest of the company is: Why do we want to do this? What are our objectives? Typically, the following objectives justify a special executive compensation program:

- to strength executives' focus on long-term versus short-term goals
- to provide executives with financial ownership opportunities
- to encourage executive retention
- to ensure that executives make a reasonable equity investment
- to prepare for an intial public offering (IPO).

There is also a special reason that is often seen in China:

- to "clean up" prior ownership commitments that were made "unofficially" to some executives in the past without clear documentation.

If a company has any of these objectives, it makes sense for it to have a special executive compensation plan.

Cash versus Stock. There are both advantages and disadvantages associated with rewarding executives with cash or stock. Chinese law complicates the stock approach, so it usually requires outside assistance, either through a law firm or a specialized executive compensation consultant, or both. Not only are the laws complex, they are also constantly changing. Furthermore, offering stock haphazardly can incur a huge tax liability to the employee, thus minimizing the financial gain.

While offering cash is a simpler approach than offering stock, it does require an immediate cash outlay. This may be a problem from a cash-flow perspective, as well as from a profit-and-loss perspective. (The new standard in the US is to charge the expense of the stock options on the balance sheet when they are granted. In China, the laws are a little less clear and so, again, I strongly recommend obtaining professional advice on whether you must expense your stock options at the time you grant them, or whether you can wait until they are exercised by the employees.)

Another argument against offering cash is that it is no different from any other bonus and does not simulate ownership. Some companies overcome this by tying the cash outlay to the stock price. In other words, just as in a stock plan, there will be no payout if the company's stock does not rise to a pre-defined amount. Also, companies that use cash for a long-term compensation plan may decide to pay out over a period of time—say, three years—in order to increase the program's employee retention value.

Differences between Western and Chinese Executive Compensation Plans

An important issue to consider when designing an executive plan in China is the relative scarcity of executive compensation market data. While the data pool is growing exponentially each year, the volume of data in China is much smaller than in other locations where executive compensation is common. As such, it is a good practice in China to collect some of your own data from competitors and/or other companies that you believe are comparable in some ways to yours. This should give you more confidence that you are doing what is common in the market than you would get from relying on a third party's market data alone. If you choose to rely also on foreign company databases, you should be aware of the following significant differences between China and elsewhere:

- Eligibility for participation in an equity plan in China tends to be reserved only for the highest executives, as compared to firms in the US, Australia, and Europe that allow eligibility for ownership at lower levels. However, multinational firms may go deeper into the firm than local firms when determining eligibility.
- The mix of performance measures in China is also slightly different from elsewhere. For example, in the West, the performance measures for executive plans tend to be primarily related to the company or the division. In China, the mix includes a large percentage of individual performance. So, while the company/individual mix in the West might be anywhere from 100:0 to 80:20, in China, it is more like 60:40.
- Grant sizes in China tend to be approximately 60 percent of those in the US.
- Around the world, there are large differences in payout schemes for executives in different industries. While some industry differences exist in China, they are not very significant.
- Grants are made less frequently in China than elsewhere. Again using the US as an example, the most common approach is a payout every year based on three-year goals. This is called a "rolling" plan. In China, the most common approach is to pay out every two years, with new goals developed at that time. This is called a "cliff" plan.

Generally, Chinese HR professionals can learn about executive compensation by studying the plan elements of other countries. If you are part of a multinational, then you may be advised to use a similar plan in China to what is used in your home office. But be cognizant of the cultural issues mentioned earlier in the chapter. What works in the US or in Europe may simply not make sense in China, and you may need to start from scratch. The main differences between Chinese executive compensation plans and those elsewhere lie not in the elements of the plan, but in the details of those elements. Thus, the leader should look very closely at eligibility, grant size, grant frequency, and the mix of performance measures to ensure that the plan makes sense in China. Again, when designing an executive compensation plan in China, it is wise to include a third party that can provide objectivity and technical expertise. Most HR professionals in China are not experienced in the special nuances of executive compensation. While all of the major HR consulting firms have expertise in executive compensation, the level of expertise varies significantly from office to office and from time to time. Good executive compensation consultants are thin on the ground and very much in demand in China, so it is prudent to do your due diligence instead of just hiring someone based on the consulting firm's reputation.

Criticism of Rewards

Perhaps the most frequently used way to influence an employee's motivation is by providing some kind of reward. This may be in the form of salary, bonus, incentive, non-cash recognition, training, mentoring, rotational assignments, and other developmental opportunities. Many scholars believe that providing such rewards to employees is a positive influence on motivation. However, there are some who disagree. They believe that external rewards, especially cash rewards, are only temporary. They may influence behavior for only a short time. Eventually, though, the influence will fade and the employee will seek a new reward for improving their performance. The late Peter Drucker was perhaps the most famous proponent of this critique.

While I am clearly a believer in providing rewards in an intelligent and strategic way, I partially agree with the critics. I believe that there are plenty of reward systems in companies that are neither strategically aligned nor integrated with other HR programs. This causes great confusion to employees and can have a demotivating influence. But well-designed programs that are tied to company objectives and are reviewed and modified annually are good for motivation. So, the very important point here is to ensure that reward programs are designed well and reviewed regularly. I have heard many managers in China ask for reward programs for their teams or divisions or companies, with no apparent concern that they are aligned with their company strategy or reflect the desired culture. This is a formula for disaster.

In the next chapter, we will look at one of the most commonly used approaches for attracting, retaining, and developing our senior-most leaders—executive coaching.

Chapter Eighteen Executive Summary

Rewarding Executives in China

- Reward programs in China are very difficult to manage. Even if the HR departments are sophisticated in compensation technology, reward program management is still complicated by the diverse needs in different geographies and the distortion caused by the supply and demand of "hotter" jobs such as computer engineers.

- Managing rewards is also complicated by the unique social status applied to salaries in China. Chinese employees will likely discuss every detail of their compensation package with their friends and family. This causes the leader and the HR department to face a level of complexity in making salary decisions that is typically not found in the West, where individual compensation is a private matter.

- Anywhere in the world, it is good practice to use compensation strategically. This means using the different elements of pay to reward different aspects of performance. Typically, base salary is used to compensate for basic qualification for the job and daily performance. Annual incentive plans are for annual or other short-term goals. Executive compensation is used to reward executives for the long-term contributions they make, over and above what is provided for their daily and annual contributions.

- When considering base compensation, it is very important also to consider non-monetary awards, such as formal recognition, training and development, and special assignments, in addition to a competitive cash salary.

- For annual incentive plans, it is common practice in China to simply replicate a plan that was successful elsewhere, such as in another firm in China or in the company's own home country. But such a practice is unwise in China, where the societal culture is unique and corporate cultures vary widely from company to company. The only practice that makes sense in China is to tailor your plan to your own corporate culture and objectives.

- There are four basic elements of an annual incentive plan design. These are participation, performance measures, payout formula,

(continued)

(continued)

and administration. Each of these needs to be examined closely for the best fit in your China organization.

- Executive compensation takes into account the different kinds of contribution that executives are asked to make to a company, as compared to other employees. Essentially, the executive's impact is more strategic and longer-term. As such, it is good practice to provide additional compensation to executives to reward them for their longer-term contributions.

- There are a number of reasons for offering special compensation to executives. These include encouraging executives to be more focused on long-term goals, encouraging executive "buy-in," retaining executives, preparing for an IPO, or simply keeping your reward program competitive. Whatever the specific reasons for offering executive pay, there will be different plan elements that are suited to those objectives.

- In the West, executive compensation is often tied to the company's stock price and involves the granting of company stock. This process has special legal and tax implications in China that vary from location to location. Therefore, local counsel is necessary, in the form of compensation expertise or legal assistance, or both.

- Market practices in China for the various executive compensation pay elements differ from those found in the West. These include eligibility, payout percentages, grant amounts, and payout frequency. This is another reason not to try to do this on your own. Furthermore, most HR managers in China are not experienced enough to do this on their own.

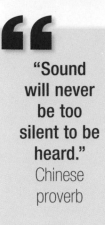

Chapter 19

EXECUTIVE COACHING

The very Western concept of executive coaching does not always fit easily in China, at least as it has been intended when introduced from the West. The Westerner sees the coaching intervention as being designed to help employees become more independent and to handle business matters more effectively. The Chinese, on the other hand, often see the coaching relationship as a paternalistic one. It is a way for collectivists to "look after their staff."[1]

Yi Min, Director of Global Leadership and Organizational Development at Lenovo, comments:

> *"Coaching does not work very well in China. We Chinese may smile on the outside about this, but we are arrogant in our hearts. Some leaders feel, 'I already know how to swim in the water. I don't need a coach to help me.'"*
>
> **Yi Min**, *Director of Global Leadership and Organization Development, Lenovo Group, Raleigh, North Carolina, United States.*

A Chinese colleague once said to me: "We Chinese can be very arrogant about coaching. We may be very polite with the coach, but the truth is, we usually don't think we need it." While this sentiment is not always true, I have experienced it myself. As an executive coach, I have often been faced with Chinese executives who were forced into a coaching agreement by their boss. My usual approach is to try to establish some credibility upfront. But if an executive truly does not want to be coached, there is little a coach can do. It will be a waste of money for the firm and a waste of time for all the parties. In the West, executive coaching is very popular and often in demand. People selected to receive coaching are often picked because they are viewed as having high potential. Coaching is intended to help them get ahead more quickly than if they are just left to themselves. In China, in my experience, coaching is mostly considered a remedial program to help those who are deficient in one or more areas become more proficient.

I remember a situation where I had been coaching a senior Chinese executive in an American firm in China. The coaching assignment was for nine months and was drawing to a close. We had made good progress helping this person to become more aware of his impact on the firm and of how others sometimes perceived his behavior as significantly different from his intentions.

Around the same time as we were terminating our coaching relationship, he had a new boss join the firm. The previous boss, who was responsible for hiring me, was a Westerner. He had a coach himself for a long time. The new boss was Chinese and not very familiar with coaching. My client introduced me to the new boss and we exchanged pleasantries. The next time we met, which was our final meeting, the client recalled the day he introduced me to the boss. He said that, after I left, the boss asked him about the coaching: "You're already doing such a good job. Why do you need a coach?" Fortunately, my client was able to explain that the coaching provided great value by way of improving his leadership style. I am not sure if the new leader was convinced.

Despite the cultural resistance, executive coaching is still one of the hottest developmental activities in China today. Why? Because companies in China realize that they are stretching their executives to do much more than they were developed for. Many of them are much younger than their Western counterparts and are not yet experienced in doing the kind of leading their firms expect of them. Secondly, most Chinese executives rose to their positions by being technically advanced in their fields, but not necessarily because they were great leaders of people. Now, these executives, who are sometimes significantly younger and less experienced than the average global executive, are being asked to do things that were never previously expected of them.

Coaching is necessary in local firms as well as in multinationals, with the latter having the added need of helping their executives to lead across cultural boundaries.

Coaching Categories

Many people in China use the term "executive coach" to describe their work. But just like the term "consultant," it can cover a wide range of activities aimed at achieving different results.

Strategy Coaching. This form of coaching is focused on helping executives to develop and implement strategy. It is often delivered by former line executives who have had experience in developing and implementing strategies in their own firms before becoming coaches. Many of these experts use specific models. The intervention is more often with teams of executives, rather than with individual executives. This type of coaching is often process-focused. It does not immediately address different leadership styles or leadership behaviors. Rather, it focuses on the desired strategy and the steps needed to bring that strategy to life. That is why it is quite common to have a strategy coach in place to work with the executive team, and a leadership coach to work with specific individuals.

Change Coaching. This form of coaching is closely related to strategy coaching. However, in this case, the organization is currently (or soon to be) in the midst of a major transition. This can mean a geographic change, a significant market expansion, a merger, or any other significant event that will lead to enormous change in the company's structure or culture. For some executives in China, this will be a first-time event and they will need coaching to help the change happen smoothly. This type of coaching is usually time-limited and is often part of an overall program of change management in the firm. The external coach may or may not be part of the larger program. In my experience in China, the internal HR department typically coordinates the overall change process. There may also be an internal team of executives that is responsible for leading this effort. Executives who benefit most from change coaching are those who are going through major changes for the first time in their business careers and may have some misgivings about the changes. It is often best that these misgivings are dealt with first, before the executives can be effective change agents themselves.

Life Coaching.   This form of coaching is much more common in the West than it is in China. But the concept is catching on in China and promises to become more important in the coming years. Coachees tend to be beginning-level executives or high-potential employees in the firm. Life coaching, also referred to as "personal development coaching" or "career coaching," is expressly focused on the needs of the individual being coached. But unlike leadership coaching, which focuses on helping the individual to become a better leader of others, life coaching is aimed at optimizing the individual's own life choices around work and career. Life coaches are also often referred to as "mentors." They may not be knowledgeable about the coachees' chosen area of work, but they focus on their development in the firm, not on their functional success there. Their main job is to help increase the coachees' self-confidence so that they can identify and reach specific personal goals. Life coaches help individuals to dream about what the future may hold for them.

Leadership Coaching.   Here the coaching intention is to help executives be better leaders of people. It usually involves some form of baseline assessment that may include a 360-degree survey to learn about the coachees' current leadership behaviors. As is often found from these assessments, the employees' perceptions of the leaders' behaviors are not always the same as the executives intended. As such, the intervention in leadership coaching is aimed first at self-awareness and then at behavioral change. Meetings are typically held monthly and may be in person or by telephone. The coaching usually lasts for a period of six to 12 months before a new assessment is conducted to see if there has been improvement in the coachees' desired behaviors.

There is often overlap among these coaching areas. However, it is important to identify the coach's primary focus before making a selection, so that you can match the coach with the desired needs of your firm.

How to Select a Coach to Match Your Corporate Needs

Once you have decided on why you want a coach, the choice of the coaching category is easy. But you still have work to do. How can you be sure that this particular coach will work well with your executives? In coaching, there must be chemistry between the coach and the coachee. Rather than jumping into a long-term contract, I recommend that the arrangement begin with a short-term trial period. This can be anywhere from one to three months. Of course, you will need to pay the coach for his or her work during this period, but you need not involve yourself in a long-term contract that may fail because of the poor relationship between parties. In my own work, I always suggest to the client that I get a chance to review material about the coachee and have at least one face-to-face meeting before we engage in a full contract. I do not want to waste my time any more than the client should want to waste his or her money.

Key Competencies for an Executive Leadership Coach in China

If you have decided that one or more of your executives could benefit from a leadership coach to help them better understand and improve upon their leadership behaviors, I recommend that your company's coach have the following competencies.

China Knowledge. As this book has emphasized, leading in China is very different from leading in the West. Therefore, any coach in China should be fairly knowledgeable about how business is conducted here, how Chinese employees view their executives and what they expect from them, what motivates Chinese employees, and what Western practices need to be modified to be effective here. If the coach is Chinese, you can expect that he or she already knows these things. If your company is a multinational, however, you need to be sure that the Chinese coach is familiar with the functioning of a multinational firm in China.

Self-Awareness. Just as it is important for the coach to help executives improve their self-awareness, it is imperative that the coach also be extremely self-aware. One of the things I learned many years ago when I was a psychotherapist was how to distinguish my own feelings and needs from those of the clients. I believe that one of the key weaknesses in some of the coaches I have met in China was that their own needs got in the way of the clients' needs. Coaches in China need to put their clients first, even when it means that the coach's action could lead to him or her being fired. If the action is taken with a client's best interests in mind, then being fired is a justifiable outcome. When interviewing a possible coach, I suggest you ask the coach questions about his or her coaching intentions, reasons for being a coach, and expectations about success. If the answers lean more toward the coach than the client, I suggest you look for a different coach.

Listening Skills. Coaches need to be better listeners than talkers. While beginning coachees often prefer to listen to their coaches, that approach will not help develop the coachees quickly. Coaches need to spend time listening for clues from their coachees about their most pressing issues, especially if the coachees don't appear to know what their own biggest needs are. One of the challenges for coaches in China is to resist the temptation to do most of the talking and to be offering advice. Generally, Chinese employees are very respectful of coaches, especially if they are older and more experienced. Employees genuinely believe that they can best learn and develop if they listen to these experts and follow their advice. But research has shown clearly and often that the most permanent positive change in coaching relationships will happen when the coachees are able to identify their issues, reflect on these, and suggest their own solutions. A coach's job is to help coachees clarify the issues, raise their consciousness about their importance, and prioritize solutions.

Trustworthiness.   In my experience, it usually takes at least two or three live meetings before coachees begin really to trust their coaches. As described in earlier chapters, personal trust is a very important part of the culture in China. Some coaches in other countries may feel they can get right down to business with coachees at the first meeting because they have such great reputations. But in China, trust must be earned over time. As such, coaches need to demonstrate their trustworthiness early on. They do this by listening carefully and responding to real needs (as noted above), by setting ground rules with coachees and sticking to those rules, and by dealing with issues of confidentiality.

Business Acumen.   No executive coach can possibly know very much about all of the varied industries in which their coachees work. But they must at least have a working knowledge of the industry, as well as the client company. Furthermore, the coach should have a pretty good understanding of the roles the coachees play in their companies, and of how those roles relate to the rest of their organizations. I recently began an engagement with a major international firm in China where I was to coach a number of executives over a one-year period. Before beginning the assignment, I participated in a one-day primer on how the firm was organized and how the various departments and functions were interrelated. I volunteered my time for this primer because I felt it would improve my ability to be a better coach at the firm. I recommend this approach whenever a coach is being hired to work with several executives at a firm.

Intuitiveness.   Whatever is discussed in the coaching session usually just scratches the surface. The most important matters lie beneath the surface. This is where a coach earns his or her pay. The coach needs to be able to understand what is really being said and then suggest to the coachees that there may be deeper meanings to what is being said and, if true, could lead to a different way of behaving. This kind of intuitive judgment brings the coachees to higher levels of self-awareness and improved performance.

Flexibility.   Oftentimes, a plan is decided upon at one coaching session to be followed at the next session. However, when the session opens, the coach learns that another matter has emerged that is more important or more urgent than what was discussed in the original plan. While the coach needs to provide discipline and keep the coachees working in a particular direction, he or she also needs to be flexible enough to change the plan if required.

Versatility. Unless the coach specifies that he or she only works with one particular function or one particular level, the need for versatility is critical. In my practice, I may work with a CEO at one company in the morning, and then with a high-potential director in a different firm in the afternoon. It is a good practice, when interviewing coaches, to ask if they have had more or less success at particular organizational levels or functions, and then to match that coach appropriately in your firm. But when there are not that many coaches available, the best approach is to hire someone who can be versatile and work well at different levels and functions in the firm.

Remedial Coaching

If a person requires remedial coaching, it should be made clear to all parties what their specific issue is, and a contract (either verbal or written) should be established to work on this issue for a specific period of time. Coaching for remedial purposes should never be disguised as something it is not. Of course, the company and the coach need to describe the coaching in such a way that the person being coached does not lose face. For example, if a Chinese executive needs help getting accustomed to a Western firm and Western managers, coaching can help him or her to be more successful in the firm. While this may at first be seen as a problem for management, it can be turned into a very positive experience for the employee and the firm if the coaching can help him or her perform more effectively.

True developmental coaching for high-potential executives is a very different matter. Here the contract may be for a defined time or it may be open-ended. Executives selected for this kind of coaching in China should be reassured that this is a reward for their excellent performance. It is designed to help them move quickly on a fast track by improving those behaviors that have already been identified as strengths and decreasing those behaviors that could be detrimental to their careers.

The Coaching Language

As a general rule, the coach and the coachee must be able to communicate without an interpreter. I have seen exceptions to this with strategic coaching and change coaching, where the work may be more about things to do than about how one personally should behave. But in the cases of life coaching and leadership coaching, where the focus is entirely on individual behavior, I believe it is not prudent to hire a coach in a situation where an interpreter is required. Those types of coaching will be much less effective if a third party is involved. A private dyadic alliance must form between the life coach or leadership coach and the coachee in order to produce the best results. An interpreter, by definition, destroys the ability to form that alliance.

There are still only a limited number of qualified senior coaches in China, though their number will increase as the coaching field grows. But for now, companies should proceed cautiously. A bad coaching experience is worse than no coaching experience.

Finally, I recommend that the most senior executive set an example by being coached. It is much easier for a leader to justify the use of coaching if he or she is also a coaching client.

In the third and final part of the book, we turn to what must be done next to ensure that leadership in China can be continuously improved.

Note

1 Romie F. Littrell, "Desirable Leadership Behaviors of Multi-Cultural Managers in China," *Journal of Management Development*, Vol. 21, No. 1, 2002, pp. 5–74 at p. 42.

Chapter Nineteen Executive Summary

Executive Coaching

- Executive coaching is not as common in China as in the West.

- In the West, coaching is most often used as a reward for successful executives to help them move up the corporate structure as rapidly as possible. In China, coaching is more often used for remedial purposes. It is very important for the leader hiring the coach, as well as for the coach, to make it clear to the coachee the purpose of the coaching assignment.

- There are different kinds of executive coaching available, and so the leader and the HR department need to be sure they are getting what they need in a coach. The different types of coaching, are strategy coaching, change coaching, life coaching, and leadership coaching.

- A trial period with the coach is a recommended approach in China, to help the coachee feel comfortable with the coach and with the potential value of being coached before making a commitment.

- Putting a time limit on the coaching assignment reassures the coachee that the process is not open-ended, which could be considered threatening by some Chinese executives who do not want to be seen as always needing this kind of external help.

- Important competencies for leadership coaches in China include: China knowledge, self-awareness, listening skills, trustworthiness, business acumen, intuitiveness, flexibility, and versatility.

- Having the CEO being coached as well helps set the tone for coaching in the firm. It is much easier for a leader to hire a coach for a subordinate executive if the CEO is also a coachee.

WHAT DO WE DO NOW?

"Away with your dualism, your likes and dislikes.
Every single thing is just one mind."
Huang Po, Chinese Buddhist philosopher

Introduction to Part III

Part III is the most theoretical part of the book. It begins with Chapter Twenty, which examines what a comprehensive leadership program might look like in a company operating in China. The chapter first describes the necessary elements for a leadership program and why there are special considerations for developing them in China. It also reviews the various elements of a comprehensive leadership program and suggests how they can be introduced in China. Finally, it examines how China's leaders are at different developmental levels and gives suggestions on how to segment your leadership programs.

The next chapter suggests how a Chinese manager can progress to being a global leader. This is an issue for many managers themselves, as well as for their companies.

The final chapter takes a look at what the future holds for leadership in China. How does the rapid change going on in China now impact leaders there? What further research is required to round out the story? How well do existing popular research models apply in China? Are there any parts to these models that can be applied directly without modification, or do they require being tailored to a Chinese approach in their entirety? Are there already new ways of examining cultural differences within China?

The chapters in this part are written for designers of leadership programs, or for scholars wishing to undertake new research in order to better understand the subject. Part III does not follow the more practical approach taken in Part II, which is clearly aimed at the practitioner. In other words, it is aimed at those who are concerned more with how to improve leadership in China overall, and less with how to lead as an individual.

Chapter 20

WHAT SHOULD A LEADERSHIP PROGRAM IN CHINA LOOK LIKE?

Even when one thinks one knows the "right" way to do something, there still might be a better way. In my experience with "corporate China," I have heard of many cases where companies have claimed to have "solid" leadership programs. Many of these programs, however, consist of nothing more than focused training for people who are either currently filling leadership roles or are expected to do so within a few years. While such intervention may bear fruit, it is not a comprehensive leadership program.

Actually, very few companies in the world have such programs. Many firms in China have good intentions and combine some of the key elements of developing leaders in their programs. But rarely have I seen a firm here that encompasses all of what is needed to build, develop, and retain its key leaders.

In fairness to Chinese firms, there are unique features of doing business in China that make it tougher than elsewhere to do this. While companies around the globe are frustrated by an overemphasis on short-term operations, the fanatical desire for quick profits in China makes a long-term investment such as leadership development a difficult program to sell. Furthermore, most current Chinese leaders got to their positions by fighting and scraping their way to the top. There were rarely any programs to help them get there. As one Chinese executive told me recently, "We throw the high potentials into the water. The ones who swim the fastest and the furthest get promoted." While this process of elimination may work in the short term, it assumes an endless flow of new talent. But as we know, while there are many, many people in China, the percentage qualified to work in our best firms is small. Leaders cannot afford to lose the good ones to other firms that may be more willing to develop future leaders.

More importantly, this "sink or swim" mentality also runs counter to the understanding that we can "teach" people to swim better. If we do this early enough, we can help many more to swim faster and farther than they would if we did not provide that help. That is what a leadership program is designed to do.

A Comprehensive Leadership Program in China

A comprehensive leadership program in China should consist of four major parts: a program *strategy*; a method of *identifying* future leaders; a *development* program for both potential and current leaders; and a *retention* program for current leaders.

Leadership Strategy.   Every company needs leaders. The questions they must answer are: How many leaders do we need, and at what levels—entry, intermediate, and senior? Is there a gap between our current internal pipeline and our future needs? How do we fill that gap?

Some human resources directors in China have told me that a strategy for leadership development is not necessary. They argue that, for the foreseeable future, they just need to develop as many leaders as they can, because the demand is endless and the supply is limited. That may be true, but it does not eliminate the need to get answers to the above questions so that your program has a clear direction and measurable goals. This is your roadmap. It is not difficult to do, even if most of the answers you come up with are best guesses from a collection of current senior executives. How do you know if you will arrive at the right place if you don't know where you are going?

Development Dimensions International (DDI) found that more than one-half of Chinese leaders are inadequately prepared for their roles in the new economy. As they note, "New leaders are thrown into their roles with little or no preparation. New leaders may be selected because they are good at technical aspects of their jobs, but not necessarily at leading people."[1]

Robert Gandossy and Mark Effron, in their book *Leading the Way*, have identified what they consider to be the "three truths" of developing leaders. These are: (1) leadership from the top; (2) a maniacal focus on the best talent; and (3) doing the right programs the right way.[2]

The first truth, "leadership from the top," is not only about providing words of support; it also guarantees that the "top" of the firm offers resources (people, time, and money) to ensure that leadership programs can be carried out. It also means that the board of directors will support the leadership effort, including board members' own appraisals of existing leaders.[3]

The second truth, "a maniacal focus on the best talent," means that you will focus strongly on those people you have identified as the future leaders of the firm. This may be through a "high-potential program" or some other program that identifies top talent, recognizes them for their future potential as leaders, offers them different types of assignments that include heightened account-abilities, and rewards them differently than average employees.[4]

Thirdly, the authors emphasize the importance of "doing the right programs the right way."[5] Examples of what some of these programs might look like are given later in this chapter.

Identifying Future Leaders. To ensure that you are able to keep your China leadership pipeline fresh, you need to have at least two programs and they must both be done well. They are: a "succession-planning program" and a "high-potential program." They should both be linked to competencies. It won't matter if your company does not have a full, corporate-wide competency program in place. What *is* necessary, though, is that you have identified the three to five key leadership competencies in your firm in China, and that you carefully select for these as you are planning succession or deciding who should be in a high-potential program. Good business results may get a person noticed, but the presence of the right competencies will almost always guarantee leadership success in your firm.

A basic succession-planning program in China should at least identify the top positions reporting to the CEO and have potential replacements identified for each of those. (The best international practice is to go two to three levels down from the CEO and have at least two candidates for each of those positions. But I believe this type of program is currently unreachable in China because of the scarcity of leadership talent.)

A common debate within businesses around the world, which is also often found in China, is whether to select future leaders from inside or outside the firm. Murray Dalziel, Group Managing Director for Global Practice at the Hay Group, says that a mix is best. "If you get all the talent from within, there will be a tendency toward inward-thinking. … But if all the talent comes from outside, it's extremely hard to gel."[6]

As for a high-potential program in China, there is much to consider. It should at least do the following. It should exude enthusiasm. It should use valid selection techniques and have a very transparent selection process. It should include different opportunities for people selected than for the general population, and it should also offer different rewards based on their new accountabilities. Finally, it should not be kept secret. Everyone should know that such a program exists and what it would take to be selected. I am not suggesting that all of the program members should be publicly listed, but the method of selection and the requirements for being admitted to the program *should* be.

With these "succession-planning" and "high-potential" programs in place, a company can best identify its future China leaders. Such programs, combined with the supply–demand analysis mentioned above, can help the firm decide whether to stay internal for future leadership promotions or to go outside.

Leadership Development. There are numerous components to a leadership development program. A company need not have them all, but the more you do have, the more likely it is you will reach people in ways that will help them be better leaders. A. G. Lafley, CEO of Procter & Gamble, estimates that he spends one-third to one-half of his time on leadership development.[7] Common leadership development programs include: mentoring personal development, coaching, training, developmental assignments, key project teams (action learning), rotational assignments, and global assignments. As a result of the relative inexperience of many HR professionals in China, and the comparative rarity of some of these programs there, many companies in China tend to lag behind other countries in the sophistication of these programs.

The first two leadership development items listed (mentoring and coaching) are sometimes confusing and may initially be used interchangeably. In fact, many people use the two words as synonyms, when they actually have different meanings. A mentor is someone who is not necessarily an expert in the mentee's specific work field. Rather, the mentor is assigned, because of his or her wisdom and experience, to help guide a junior employee through the corporate maze. The English word "mentor" is derived from ancient Greece. The Greek king Odysseus was going off to war and needed someone to look after his son while he was gone. He wanted someone who could guide his son in the various ways of the world as he grew and developed. The person he chose was named Mentor.

A "coach," on the other hand, is an expert. The expertise is often in the coachee's work field. This coach is usually the manager, or some other senior expert selected by the manager, whose job is to help develop new employee skills. But the coach can also be in football or tennis or, in the case of business, leadership development.

With that distinction understood, let us say something about each of these developmental elements.

Mentoring for personal development means that the company will assign someone, usually an internal resource, to work with the employee to develop himself or herself inside the firm. The mentor is like a trusted aunt or uncle. Discussions are not technical, but instead are focused on what steps a future leader could take to be most successful in his or her career. The success of these programs requires both the mentor and the mentee to be committed to making it work. The HR department can often help here by checking in occasionally with both parties to make sure the relationship is moving ahead as it should.

Leadership coaching usually involves an outsider and is most often reserved for the most senior leaders. It can be expensive, and the company needs to do a cost-benefit analysis in each case. A range of professionals may call themselves leadership coaches.

Some focus on personal leadership development, some on corporate strategy, and others on change management, while some are experts in particular corporate functions. A company needs to be sure that the coach it selects is suited to providing the results it expects from the coaching.

Oftentimes, the coach will use a formal assessment instrument to help identify the leadership styles and leadership behaviors that the leader employs. Some behaviors are very constructive, while others may be destructive, possibly even to the point of derailing the leader's career. The assessment instrument helps the leader to identify these behaviors, and to strengthen the former and minimize the latter. Furthermore, if the instrument applies a 360-degree approach, the leader can learn whether others view his or her intended behaviors in the same way as they are intended. For example, some leaders, in their haste to teach others the "best way" to do something, may be viewed by those others as being perfectionistic and therefore impossible to please.

Developmental assignments are usually short-term and involve doing something that the employee typically would not be asked to do in their normal work activities. For example, a young engineer may temporarily be assigned to the HR department to get a feel for the kind of people issues that the company faces every day. A person in sales or manufacturing may be assigned to the finance department in order to see the world from a non-line perspective, and to get a better idea of how costs enter into the corporate equation. Sometimes, an employee receives a developmental assignment in addition to his or her regular duties. For example, the employee may work in his or her engineering role for 80 percent of the time and in an administrative staff function for the remaining 20 percent.

Working on a *key project team* is also time-limited and allows the employee to do something in conjunction with others from different functions and often from different locales. This type of work is designed to teach teamwork, as well as how to operate across boundaries.

Rotational assignments provide a way to give two or more employees the chance to learn something different without having to leave the firm to do so. It also helps to build cross-functional teamwork because the rotated employees bring with them the knowledge and networks of previous teams. A software company in Shanghai that is having difficulty with cross-functional teamwork is using rotational assignments to break the bonds formed in very small teams and extend those to broader teams. The company believes that rotating team leaders as well as individual team members is a healthy way to keep people excited and to remain focused on the bigger picture, rather than just on their smaller teams.

Global assignments are very important for teaching people how things work in different cultures, and also for enhancing their networks. This is particularly important in China, since most Chinese employees have never worked abroad. A typical arrangement for a multinational firm in China is to send the Chinese employee to the corporate headquarters for six to 12 months. This will almost always improve the employee's ability to understand the workings of the firm. It also extends the employee's network and, perhaps most importantly for China, gives the other employees at the head-quarters an opportunity to better understand their China operations.

Leadership Retention. One executive in China told me that his company leaves "on the table" at least RMB10 million (more than US$1.4 million) every year because they do not have the leadership talent to go and get it. Having enough good leaders is not just a human resources department challenge. This is a critical business need, and companies cannot afford to lose the leaders they already have. This is why leadership retention must be a part of your program. It is not enough just to find and develop leaders. You must also have a plan for retaining them.

Among the best practices for retaining leaders are the following: opportunities for advancement, recognition from the top, and compensation. Many books on human resources have stressed the logistical and financial importance of employee retention, so there is no need to repeat it here. I will mention, however, that compensation plays a much bigger part at the executive level than lower down in the organization. As most business people already know, compensation is usually not the key element for retention. However, with top jobs in the firm, its relative importance increases. Good leaders can demand very high salary packages in the market. These jobs are so important that a competitor will not hesitate to offer a huge increase to try and attract an effective leader. As such, if your leader is a good one, I recommend a pay package closer to the 75th percentile than the 50th. The same argument could be made for many non-executive jobs in China, unlike elsewhere in the world. As noted in an earlier chapter, salary has a very high social status value as well as filling an economic need. Furthermore, in some high-growth financial areas such as Shanghai, the importance of salary is multiplied because of the relatively high cost of living, especially in terms of housing.

A Further Thought on Leadership in China

Another area to consider when developing leaders is the different needs of people at different levels of the firm. The junior leader will typically lead a function or a team. This person may need many of the basic skills of leadership, such as decision-making, talent management, organizational finance, and organizational design. Much of this can be obtained through training, coaching, and developmental assignments. Mid-level leaders need to understand how to manage across organizational boundaries. The employees need to learn about cultural differences, as well as business differences among departments and in different geographical areas. This type of development is best obtained through rotational assignments, global assignments, and serving on key project teams, especially those that are cross-functional. Finally, the senior-most leaders need to develop strategically. This is best developed through external coaching.

Notes

1   Paul R. Bernthal, Jason Bondra, and Wei Wang, *Leadership in China* (Pittsburgh, PA: Development Decisions International, 2005), p. 11.
2   Robert Gandossy and Mark Effron, *Leading the Way* (Hoboken, NJ: John Wiley & Sons, 2004).
3   *Ibid.*, pp. 25–44.
4   *Ibid.*, pp. 49–70.
5   *Ibid.*, pp. 73–108.
6   William J. Holstein, "Best Companies for Leaders," *Chief Executive*, November 2005.
7   *Ibid.*, p. 25.

Chapter Twenty Executive Summary

What Should a Leadership Program in China Look Like?

- Many companies in China say they have "leadership development programs," when in fact they have a series of training programs for existing or future leaders.

- A comprehensive leadership program should contain four elements: a program *strategy*; a method of *identifying* future leaders; a *development* program for both potential and current leaders; and a *retention* program for current leaders.

- The strategy should include a method for finding leaders both in the firm and outside. It should also identify what programs will be included and how they will be executed.

- Identification of future leaders can come from both a succession-planning program and some form of high-potential program.

- The development program may contain such interventions as mentoring, coaching, developmental assignments, rotational assignments, and global assignments.

- Leadership retention is a major cost item for companies in China. While retention is not related only to rewards, it has a very high correlation in China. Therefore, leaders need to pay special attention to the reward programs of the best employees, especially those who are likely to become future leaders in the firm.

- Leadership programs need to differentiate between leaders at different levels. Beginning leaders need functional expertise, much of which can be obtained through training. Mid-level leaders need access to programs that help them lead across corporate and geographic boundaries. This is usually obtained through special programs and assignments. The most senior leaders need development in strategic thinking and leadership behaviors, and these are most often offered through executive coaching.

> "When planning for a year, plant corn. When planning for a decade, plant trees. When planning for life, train and educate people."
> Guan Zhong, Chinese philosopher

Chapter 21

PROGRESSING FROM A CHINESE MANAGER TO A GLOBAL LEADER

A question that is uppermost in the minds of many Chinese managers today is: "What do I need to do to become a global leader in this firm?" Likewise, many corporate leaders are asking: "How can we develop our high-potential Chinese managers to become global leaders?" This chapter attempts to answer these questions.

This issue is so common in China today, that I once thought of writing an entire book on the subject. I wanted to interview as many Chinese global leaders as I could find, to learn first hand how they had made the transition to the world stage. As I looked for possible subjects, however, I found that such managers were very few in number. Most Chinese executives I spoke with could not think of even one. Managers of Chinese firms that have expanded abroad may not necessarily be considered global leaders unless they are savvy enough to do business successfully in their adopted foreign country. In fact, many Chinese firms that expand abroad are required to localize their leadership in order to survive.

Most foreign companies operating in China also have yet to solve the problem of how to elevate their Chinese managers who want to take on global responsibility. Many Chinese managers believe the problem lies not in their own capabilities, or the lack thereof, but in the existence of other barriers to promotion to the world stage.

At one foreign firm where I was conducting a workshop with Chinese managers in 2009, a participant commented that the only way he could get a global leadership role in the firm would be by changing his passport. He described a pattern of corporate prejudice at the firm against Chinese employees taking on leadership roles outside of China. Several of his colleagues in the workshop agreed that they felt there was a "glass ceiling" that prevented them from moving ahead because they are Chinese.

I think there are two possible responses to this manager's complaint. The first is to acknowledge that, in many foreign firms based in China, there is indeed a "glass ceiling" in place. The home country executives may feel more comfortable working with people they have known for a long time and whose values they share. So, it is common to see a homogeneous senior management team in global leadership positions. This is true not only in the West, but also in Japan, India, Korea, and even China.

But I prefer the second possible response, which offers more hope for Chinese employees: The future of business lies in Asia. China is at the head of the pack right now, and most foreign leaders understand that many of the future global leaders of their firms will come from China. It simply comes down to numbers. The timing may not be as rapid as some Chinese managers would like, but it is inevitable. Chinese managers must develop patience along with ambition.

Most foreign executives in China would dispute that their firms are prejudiced against developing local managers into global leaders. It may be purely a business decision based on the fact that most of their Chinese employees do not yet have the experience or the traits that the firm requires to work abroad, especially in a leadership position. Having discussed this issue with many foreign executives, I do not belief there is a general prejudice in most foreign firms against Chinese managers. Nevertheless, the sentiment cannot be disregarded since it is a perception held by many Chinese employees.

A European company that operates in various locations in China was building a very large new plant. Back at its headquarters, the firm's top management said that they wanted the new plant manager to be a European, because the job required regular contact with executives in the home country. The job also required the management of European employees in China. The leaders in China, however (who were also European), had a different view. They had selected a local Chinese employee who they felt had the traits required to do the job. While he had not yet worked abroad, and he was not familiar with managing foreigners, the China leaders believed it would be best for the firm to put him in the job. It was thought his promotion would raise morale among the other Chinese employees and also be a valuable development opportunity for the candidate.

In order to smooth the way, however, I was hired to coach this very bright and relatively young Chinese executive. The coaching focused on several areas: building his self-confidence; increasing his understanding of the differences involved in working with foreign, compared to Chinese, employees; encouraging him to adopt a more extroverted style than was naturally comfortable for him; and achieving a better understanding of his leadership styles and how they were perceived by others (especially foreigners), so that he could work on adjusting these styles to achieve a better fit with his new role as a global executive. I am happy to say that, according to all involved, the candidate was able to do what he needed to do to be successful in his new role. While this is not the same as leading abroad, the executive's regular contact and negotiations with the home country are a very positive first step for this firm in their desire to transform Chinese managers into global leaders.

Let's take a look at some of the barriers facing Chinese managers today.

Barriers to Going Global

From my observation, there are several key barriers that Chinese managers who wish to go global must overcome. Some of these are experiential. In order to be a global leader, most firms will require that you have at least worked abroad for a period of time so that you have developed some level of intercultural sensitivity. The number of Chinese managers who have already had some level of international work experience or education is quite low. So, before we will see a groundswell of Chinese managers moving on to global leadership positions, we simply need more time. Firms in China (both foreign and local Chinese) are beginning to develop the means to send employees abroad to learn the ropes of foreign business. This is easier for foreign firms, as they have an offshore headquarters where employees can be sent to learn in a fairly protected environment. For the locally headquartered Chinese firms, however, the challenge is greater. In most cases, when they send employees abroad, they are sending them to locations where the firm does not have much experience with the local culture. These Chinese managers have to learn on their own. Some Chinese companies are developing on-boarding programs in foreign countries for their Chinese expatriates. But to date, these programs are few and far between and, in some firms, inconsistent from location to location.

A second barrier is a pragmatic one. It is often difficult to convince a Chinese employee to move abroad. First of all, many Chinese employees have no wish to be transferred away from China and thus see taking a temporary assignment abroad as a major sacrifice. There are issues for them of cost, schooling for their children, food choices, and more. Certainly, these are issues for any expatriate from any country. But for many Chinese, these are particularly difficult choices because of the long-held cultural belief that doing the same thing over and over again is safer and more desirable than making dramatic changes. Many managers in China have told me that it is still a difficult problem for them to convince those employees they want to send abroad to actually go. However, the number of Chinese who are bucking this trend and are choosing to study or work abroad appears to be growing.

Perhaps the biggest barriers to going global are cultural issues. Foreign cultural traits that are unfamiliar to the average Chinese manager include: being extroverted; being willing and able to challenge the boss, and to do so publicly when appropriate; respecting work–life balance; and being responsible for developing others to become future leaders. There is interesting research from the University of Science and Technology in China indicating that the Chinese are more likely to use their right brain than their left one.[1] The right brain is intuitive, while the left side of the brain is logical. This finding suggests a theory as to why some Chinese leaders may take longer than Westerners to make decisions and implement strategies. Basically, they may be processing much more information than their Western counterparts. Westerners go easily from *a* to *b* to *c*. Chinese, on the other hand, may go from *a* to *c* to *b* and then back to *a*. (The discussion in Chapter Six on *wu* (悟) and *zhong yong* (中庸) is relevant here.)

Related to these cultural issues is the development of traits that are required in Western firms, but are often not found in China. These include strategic thinking, managing across global barriers, emotional intelligence, authoritative style, and an ability to develop and articulate a vision.

Charles Shao, Director of Leadership Consulting for Hewitt Associates in Beijing, echoes the point about the lack of strategic thinking among Chinese leaders, which he attributes to the Chinese education system.

> *"Our leaders need to be more strategic in their thinking if they are to succeed abroad. Many of them have not yet seen all of the possible economic cycles that a company can go through. Therefore, they tend to act on instinct and focus on the short term rather than understanding what might happen in the long term. This is also the fault of our education system, which does not require people to think independently. Rather, they are taught what to say and when to say it. Strategic thinking first requires independent thinking."*
>
> **Charles Shao**, Director of Leadership Consulting, Hewitt Associates, Beijing, China.

Another missing ingredient, also related to culture and competency, is the ability to communicate. Global leaders are often in the public eye. Chinese leaders who have risen through the ranks based on their technical competence can no longer simply play the role of technical expert and think that this will lead to their success as a global leader. They will now be required to tell their workers, their customers, and the media why their company is the right company for this place and time. That is not something that Chinese business leaders are typically used to doing.

Overcoming these cultural issues, including developing leadership traits and communication skills, will take time. Therefore, time is the biggest obstacle facing Chinese leaders today. While, today, relatively few Chinese managers have any experience outside of China, that situation is changing. It may change sooner, rather than later, and sooner than in most other countries.

Help from within the Company

Here are a few suggestions as to how a company can help its Chinese managers progress more quickly toward global leadership.

Global Assignments. These do not have to be very long in duration; six months will do. Of course, a longer assignment is preferable. Such an assignment provides the employee with first-hand experience of working in a different culture and, if it is successful, will give him or her a newfound international perspective on business.

More on this subject from Charles Shao.

> *"Many of our leaders are very well educated. But to become a global leader, it is imperative that they first have a chance to spend time abroad in a temporary assignment where they can become accustomed to, and comfortable with, working outside of China. Some of these people may learn during the temporary assignment that they are better off in China and so decline future offers to lead globally. This is a much better outcome than sending a person abroad for the first time, giving them a leadership position, and watching them fail. If that happens, it is a disaster."*
>
> **Charles Shao**, Director of Leadership Consulting, Hewitt Associates, Beijing, China.

Coaching and Mentoring. Anyone who has not yet worked abroad or with foreign employees can benefit from the experience gained by someone else who has done so. Intervention by a coach with global leadership expertise, or by a mentor who has previously worked abroad, should be able to provide answers to any questions the employee may have, as well as objective feedback on their behavior or management style.

Leadership Development. Employees who are identified as future global leaders will need general training in global leadership. Content could include cross-cultural sensitivity, competency development, action learning projects, and emotional intelligence.

Interpersonal Skills Development. Many high-potential global leaders need to improve their language abilities, and communication and presentation skills. Most of this can be learned (American versus British use) through online training, with opportunities to practice on the job as well as in leadership development programs.

Note

1 Editor, "Chinese Use More Right Brain than Westerners," NEWSGD.com, December 22, 2006.

Chapter Twenty-One Executive Summary

Progressing from a Chinese Manager to a Global Leader

- The subject of this chapter is one that often arises when discussing career opportunities with Chinese managers. It is also an important subject for existing foreign leaders in China who are looking to take advantage of their Chinese talent and make them available for global positions.

- Many Chinese managers believe there is a "glass ceiling" that prevents them from progressing from being a local manager to a global leader. Many foreign leaders would argue that the barrier to advancement is related to traits and skills that the firm requires for global advancement, and that these traits are rarely found in the current crop of Chinese managers.

- Traits and skills that are required by Western firms for global leadership positions are: an extroverted style demonstrated with employees; excellent communication skills; an ability to think strategically; a readiness to challenge senior management; management experience across global boundaries; emotional intelligence; and a strong ability to set and articulate a corporate vision. The perception by most foreign headquarters is that their Chinese employees are still lacking in proficiency in these traits and skills.

- Programs that have been found to be useful in developing these globally required traits include: global assignments, coaching and mentoring, leadership development programs, and interpersonal skills training.

> "It does not matter if the cat is black or white, so long as it can catch mice."
> Deng Xiaoping

Chapter 22

CONCLUSION

The famous Deng Xiaoping quote noted above nicely captures the openness to new ideas found in China today. As Chinese society has moved away from the rigidity of the Mao period, it has become much more flexible and practical. Absolute "right" ways to do something have slowly been replaced by the "best" ways. It is within this framework that new methods of leading businesses can flourish. If companies in China can blend best Western practices with already understood Chinese methods, there is indeed the possibility of a successful future for these firms and a better work environment for their employees.

As many Westerners before me have observed, the more time you spend in China, the more you realize how little you know and understand. Actually, I suggest that the same can be said for Chinese people. This is an extremely complicated society for anyone to understand. The country's history is long and diverse. Recently, I read a book about Nanjing. I concluded that the history of this medium-sized city in China was as rich and complex as that of many countries. The interplay over time between the various locations in China, the numerous empires that ruled different parts of the country at different times, the huge number of diverse cultural groups, and the enormous outside influences that have touched different parts of China at different times, make the country impossible to fully comprehend.

So, anyone who ventures to write a book about China must do so with humility. To think that one can do more than scratch the surface is either misinformed or delusional. I hope I am neither. Therefore, I state emphatically that this book only scratches the surface. What follows are a few ideas for further work that would add valuable information to the topic of business leadership in China.

China is Changing Rapidly

It has been noted earlier that younger people in China lean more toward Western approaches than do older people. Obviously, most of the leaders in China are older than the average employee and so many embrace the more traditional Chinese approaches to leadership. We can only guess how the younger generation will act when it begins to run the majority of companies. However, most China experts agree that the business climate is gradually becoming more Westernized. Therefore, although I expect successful Chinese business leaders to continue to blend best Western practices with traditional Chinese thinking, the trend is in the direction of the more mature Western companies.

The other major Chinese-specific change issue is that of mobility. Historically, Chinese people did not move too far from their birthplaces. This stability has led to local cultural nuances in the various geographies of China. That is the case in business leadership as well. However, China is now seeing more mobility among its citizens, especially among those who work for large corporations. As such, I believe we will see more of a blending of China's different internal cultures than is presently the case. In my experience in cities such as Shanghai and Beijing, most of the local leaders have come from elsewhere in China. But as one moves into the outer provinces, that is not the case. Most of the leaders in Kunming, Chengdu, Xiamen, and other second- and third-tier cities were born and raised in those cities. I believe that this will soon change, too, leading to a blending of cultures in business leadership in those cities as well.

China is indeed a country in transition. It is modernizing at a pace never seen before in the world. It is rapidly moving from a primarily agricultural nation to an industrialized one. Most importantly for the subject of this book, it has moved from a planned economy to a market economy. All of these changes have been huge and rapid. Few people expect this pace of change to slow down anytime soon. As China integrates itself more and more into the global economy, we should see its companies begin to behave more like those that have been dominant in the West. However, we must also expect that the most successful Chinese leaders, at least for the next decade or so, will continue to modify Western practices to create a better fit with China's traditional wisdom and cultural practices.

The Need for Further Research

Business leadership is just one tiny aspect of Chinese society, but even this can go much deeper than what is found in this book. For example, if all the leaders interviewed for this book were from Chengdu or Dalian or Fuzhou or Kunming, how might their stories be different? Would the competencies they identified be the same ones that the primarily Beijing and Shanghai interviewees spoke of?

If we developed a questionnaire about business leadership differences in China and distributed it to 1,000 leaders from all around the country, might we not only find geographic differences, but also statistically significant differences between people who have lived in China their whole lives as compared to those who have studied abroad and then returned—the so-called *hai gui* or sea turtles (海龟)? Would there be significantly different responses between Chinese leaders from Hong Kong, Taiwan, and/or Singapore as compared to those from the Chinese mainland? Would women leaders respond very differently from their male counterparts?

Such a research project could provide a depth of information about Chinese business leadership that this book does not address. To my knowledge, such information does not yet exist in any robust form.

The Need to Test Western Leadership Models

As noted in the first chapter of this book, there have been countless books written on leadership. Many of these have been "bestsellers" in the West. But how do the principles put forward in these books fare in China? One of the top such books is *Leadership Challenge* by James Kouzes and Barry Posner.[1] The book has sold more than a million copies and there have been numerous translations to other languages. The authors espouse a leadership model that has become famous around the world. Their model states that there are five practices for exemplary leadership. They label these as follows: (1) model the way; (2) inspire a shared vision; (3) challenge the process; (4) enable others to act; and (5) encourage the heart. I have heard some experts contend that these practices are valid everywhere in the world where there are companies that must be led. It would be very useful to test these premises in China to determine if they can work there as is, or if they should be modified.

In a brief study of the Kouzes and Posner leadership model conducted in 2004, Elizabeth Weldon generated a list of questions based on behaviors she believed leaders must follow to implement each of the five Kouzes and Posner practices.[2] She then developed a questionnaire that she administered to over 100 Chinese managers. Weldon concluded that there were some similarities among these managers to the Kouzes and Posner model, but also some notable differences. For example, the Kouzes and Posner model proposes that the leader help others to succeed (enable others to act). Chinese managers in the Weldon study believed this was only of secondary importance.[3] Also, Weldon found that Chinese managers in her study were much less willing to experiment and take risks than the Kouzes and Posner model calls for.[4]

Based on the interviews completed for this book, I would make the following suggestions about the applicability of Kouzes and Posner's model in China. Successful managers in China achieve their success by proving their abilities and setting the pace for good and hard work. So, practice one, "model the way," works very well in China. "Inspiring a shared vision" is also something that Chinese leaders can identify with, although they may inspire others more by what they do, than by what they say, as many Westerners might. The idea of a "shared" vision especially rings true in China, as it implies a collective ownership rather than one that seems to come from an individual leader. However, as noted by Weldon, this was more common among multinational company leaders than among those who led in state-owned enterprises.[5]

So, the first two practices would work very well in China. The next three practices would need modification, however. "Challenging the process" is not at all a Chinese practice. As indicated throughout this book, Chinese leaders are generally more conventional and accepting of the *status quo* than their Western counterparts. Although Chinese leaders may agree intellectually with the practice of challenging, they will be slower to do so than the *Leadership Challenge* suggests. There are good examples of Chinese leaders who have done this successfully. Liu Chuanzhi of Lenovo is one such leader. But he is an exception. It will be a while before this practice can be followed in China as well as in the West.

"Enabling others to act" is discussed at length in this book, especially in Chapter Eleven where we cover the conflict between empowerment and hierarchy. The concept of enabling (or empowering) others is very Western and is based on the assumption that individuals want to be empowered. In China, many employees are still not as comfortable with empowerment as Westerners are. While the practice is still very valid for business performance, it needs to be modified and gradually introduced for it to work well in China.

The final practice in the model, "encouraging the heart," can have mixed success in China. The practice of celebrating success is already evident in China and is well received by all. It is seen to reinforce good business performance and to help stimulate high morale. But the difference in China from the Kouzes and Posner model is that the China approach almost always celebrates team success and rarely focuses on individual excellence. In fairness to Kouzes and Posner, they too talk about developing a spirit of community.[6] This is exactly what is needed in China, so the applicability of this practice is quite strong, as long as the focus is on team encouragement rather than encouragement of the individual.

I have used *Leadership Challenge* as an example here, not because I find it flawed. On the contrary, I admire the book and the Kouzes and Posner model. I have learned a great deal from it. I refer to it often in my own practice and recommend it as a first choice to any of my coachees who want to read a book on leadership. I have used their model here as an example because I view it as perhaps the most famous in the West (or at least in the US). But, as great as it is, it still needs to be modified to be fully applicable in China.

Indeed, that has been the main premise of this book. Best Western leadership practices cannot be introduced in China without some modification. If that is true for the internationally acclaimed model espoused in *Leadership Challenge*, then it is true of any other Western book on leadership.

Leadership Development Programs in China

One of my biggest surprises working with clients in China is how many multinational companies simply import the leadership programs that worked for them in their home countries. Some of these companies even pay the cost of flying and housing executive coaches from the home countries because these coaches are successful for the companies at home. As I hope I have made very clear throughout this book, this is a foolish and extremely costly endeavor. Leaders in multinational firms in China must develop their own leadership programs with people who have China expertise. In return, Chinese employees will respect the company more and, more importantly, the programs will be more suitable for executives in China than those originally designed for Westerners.

Some day, this may change. I really do not know when. But I do know that nearly all of these Western programs, designed by Westerners for other Westerners, fail in China.

Different Aspects of Leadership Development

This book focuses on behaviors for individual leaders that are seen to be most constructive in China. There are many other subjects that leaders need to understand that were not intended to be covered in this book. These include functional knowledge, leadership strategy, and organizational structure. All of these subjects have an important place in leadership development. I am not an expert in these areas, so I will only suggest a few ideas about how to address them in China.

Functional knowledge is very specific and can be obtained through training, personal development, and coaching. What should be emphasized for leaders in China, however, is that employees will judge one's functional knowledge as perhaps the key factor that qualifies one to lead. Unlike in the West, where functional knowledge is probably only a secondary or even a tertiary consideration in selecting a leader, in China it is paramount. In fact, any leader in China will do well to demonstrate their technical know-how in order to quickly win the allegiance of their team.

By "leadership strategy," I am not referring to the leadership program development strategy that was discussed in the previous chapter. I am referring instead to the way leaders use strategy to drive their companies. Leadership strategy in China has unique requirements. First, it needs to incorporate an understanding of the complexities of the Chinese national government, as well as those of the provinces and local municipalities. Secondly, it requires a thorough acceptance of the fact that China has only recently transformed from a planned, Soviet-style economy to a market economy as seen in the West. All China business strategies must consider this when planning how they will proceed in China. Finally, the discipline of strategic thinking tends to be linear in the West. In China, it needs to be holistic. In the West, one commonly looks for root causes of problems and then tries to develop solutions to overcome them. In China, the process must be more circular and continuous. The "root causes" need to be thought of more dynamically and fluidly than the kind of static and rigid roots upon which Westerners prefer to base their solutions.

So, like Western leadership behaviors, Western strategic thinking needs to be modified if it is to be useful in China.

The process of leading organizations and developing appropriate organizational structures is also different in China than in the West. Any newer form of structure, such as a leadership matrix, for example, will be met with confusion by the Chinese, who are much more comfortable with a hierarchy.

Even in the West, matrix management is difficult to implement. In China, it is extremely so. This is because matrix management is based on a premise that goes against the fundamental Chinese value of order. Remember the earlier quote from Confucius: "There is order when the king is king, the minister is minister, the father is father, and the son is son." Just as described in Chapter Eleven on empowerment, matrix management strongly threatens the entrenched Chinese desire for a hierarchical order.

Therefore, introducing unique organizational structures in China first requires recognition that anything other than a hierarchy can lead to confusion. If such a structure is applied haphazardly, it can lead to chaos.

Understanding Cultural Differences

Much of this book makes reference to broad cultural differences between Westerners and Chinese, such as individualism *versus* collectivism and low/high power-distance. Much of this language comes from cultural models designed to make such general comparisons. The prime examples used in this book are espoused by Hofstede,[7] and the GLOBE Study by House and others.[8] But it should be noted that there are newer, more focused cultural approaches now being applied that try to get beyond the broad strokes painted by the general culture models.[9] The Earley and Ang approach argues that, in order to understand and grapple with different cultural views, a company may want to look at specific cultural elements that are shared by individuals on the team. These elements include motivation, behavior, strategy, and knowledge. Earley and Ang use the term "cultural intelligence" to describe these elements. They argue that CQ can be measured and used to determine if a person is suited to working in a globally focused company. This, of course, may include a potential leader of a multi-national firm in China, and can give the company some indication of the leader's potential to function well in a multicultural environment.

A Model for Chinese Leadership

This book examines some different views held by Chinese and Western business leaders in China. There is not yet a model (at least, that I am aware of) that incorporates the best practices from both the East and the West and that could be followed by anyone who aspires to be a great leader in China. I hope that this effort is the beginning of the development of such a model. As this book goes to press, I continue to read about exciting new research in the area.

So, this book is far from being the last word on business leadership in China. The findings here, plus those to come from other sources, will be the foundation for the development of a unique Chinese model of leadership.

Notes

1 James M. Kouzes and Barry Y. Posner, *The Leadership Challenge*, 3rd edition (San Francisco: Jossey-Bass, 2006).
2 Elizabeth Weldon, "Chinese Leadership Models," CBIZ.CN (Internet), October 28, 2004.
3 *Ibid.*, p. 2.
4 *Ibid.*, p. 1.
5 *Ibid.*
6 Kouzes and Posner, *op. cit.* p. 353.
7 Geert Hofstede, *Cultures and Organizations: Software of the Mind* (London: McGraw-Hill, 1991).
8 Robert J. House, Paul J. Hanges, *et al.*, *Culture, Leadership and Organizations* (Thousand Oaks, CA: Sage Publications, 2004).
9 P. Christopher Earley and Soon Ang, *Cultural Intelligence* (Stanford, CA: Stanford University Press, 2003).

Chapter Twenty-Two Executive Summary

Conclusion

- Given the complexity of China and its culture, it is impossible to write a truly comprehensive dissertation on such a broad topic as business leadership. At best, as is the case here, we try to scratch the surface. To go deeper, there are several things we need:

  - China-focused research that looks at leadership demographic variables such as geography, age, gender, place of higher education, and experience in the West;

  - testing of well-respected Western leadership models for their applicability in China;

  - leadership development programs designed specifically for China; and

  - scrutiny of all other leadership areas, not only the behavioral leadership discussed in this book. These areas include functional knowledge, strategic leadership, and leading in different organizational structure types.

- Cultural understanding is becoming more individual-specific to include cultural intelligence (CQ). Companies with a multi-cultural makeup or a global focus may want to examine ways to identify CQ in leadership candidates before assigning them to such positions in China.

- A specific model for leading businesses in China may soon be available. Such a model may help both Westerners and Easterners become successful leaders in China.

Appendix 1

ABOUT THE INTERVIEWEES (IN ALPHABETICAL ORDER)

Bob Aubrey, Ph.D., Chairman and Founder, Metizo, Singapore.
Dr. Aubrey is among the world's preeminent experts on personal development. He is the author or co-author of six books on the subject and countless articles and reports. He founded Metizo in 2002. Metizo is devoted to an individual's personal and career development. It is the only company in the world that provides certification in this area in both higher education and in private companies. Metizo now operates in Singapore, China, Australia, and France. In addition to running Metizo, Dr. Aubrey is a professor at Tsinghua University in Beijing and Euromed Marseille. Prior to founding Metizo, Dr. Aubrey has been both an internal and external consultant to businesses and universities, primarily in France and China.

Bin Gong, Regional HR Director, Asia Pacific, Bayer HealthCare, Hong Kong. Mr. Bin grew up in Beijing. During the Cultural Revolution, he went to the countryside in Hebei, China, to work on the farms. There was no formal schooling. He was fortunate to be selected for the first class of college students after the Cultural Revolution (Class of '77). He studied English with his uncle who had lived in the US. After graduation, he worked as an English teacher in China. When China opened the door to studying abroad, he applied and was accepted to Michigan State University in the US. He later obtained an MBA from the University of Michigan. He began working in the auto industry in the US as a business developer for China. At the time, China was still very focused on communism, especially in the northeast where Mr. Bin was doing most of his business development. It was there that he began to learn the nuances of doing business in China. He noticed that Westerners were much more casual in their approach to others—for example, in their facial expressions and shoulder shrugs. He realized that the Chinese they were negotiating with often viewed these habits as condescending and signs of indifference. While not intending to, many of these Western negotiators came across as having a feeling of superiority that worked against them in negotiations. Many of the Chinese on the other side of the negotiating tables were, like Mr. Bin, products of the Cultural Revolution, who found their common ground with peasants. Mr. Bin joined Bayer HealthCare in 2001 in the US. He currently lives in Hong Kong where he manages Bayer's Asia Pacific human resources operations.

Ruby Chen, Director of the McKinsey Leadership Institute in China, McKinsey & Company, Beijing. Ms. Chen joined McKinsey in 1992. She has worked with numerous Chinese state-owned enterprises, multinational corporations, private businesses, and family-owned conglomerates in Greater China. As such, she has observed a wide variety of leadership styles, some of which have been successful and others not. Prior to joining McKinsey, Ms. Chen worked with other international firms in China. Her undergraduate degree is from Ming Chuan University in Taiwan. She also has an advanced degree from Leicester University in the UK.

Ding Jingping, Ph.D., Senior Partner and Vice President, Pan Pacific Management Institute, Beijing. Dr. Ding has been a business consultant in Beijing since 1996. Prior to Pan Pacific, he worked with Watson Wyatt Worldwide, Andersen Consulting, and the Monitor Group. Before these multinational consulting firms, he was with the Foreign Affairs Bureau of the Chinese Academy of

Social Sciences, a top-ranked research organization and think tank in China. After spending a good part of his teen years laboring in the countryside during the Cultural Revolution, he eventually entered college in Hubei province and then obtained his M.A. and Ph.D. degrees in Economics at the Chinese Academy of Social Sciences Graduate School. During the 1980s, he was a visiting scholar in the MBA program at the Sloan School of Management at the Massachusetts Institute of Technology in the US.

Kevin Fong, President, China Automobile Association, Beijing. Mr. Fong was promoted to become CEO of the China Automobile Association (CAA) in 2006. Before that, he was the General Manager of Sales and Business Development. Prior to CAA, he worked in the UK, Hong Kong, and Vietnam. This varied international experience has alerted him to various leadership styles around the world, especially in Asia. Mr. Fong received his high school and college education in Hong Kong and Switzerland. He later received his MBA from Warwick University in the UK.

(Wallacy) Gao Yong, President, Career International, Inc., Beijing. Mr. Yong was born and raised in Liaonang province in Northeast China. He attended college in Beijing and, with one partner, founded China Career in 1996. The firm has grown from two employees to 400 and is today one of the top recruiting firms in China. It is now known as Career International and operates offices in 10 Chinese cities. In addition to recruiting at all levels in most industries, it specializes in outsourcing recruitment and temporary staffing. Revenues have grown at an average rate of 60 percent per year. Gao Yong earned an EMBA from Fordham University in Beijing in 2006. He is known nationally as a leader in the recruitment field in China.

Guo Xin, Managing Director, Greater China, Mercer Human Resource Consulting, Beijing. Mr. Guo is also the Deputy Head for Mercer's Asia Pacific operations and is a worldwide partner. He was born in the northeast of China and now lives in Beijing. Before Mercer, he was a senior consultant with Accenture. He also worked in the US as both a practitioner and a consultant. He has successfully built the Mercer organization in China since 2001. He has doubled the size of its staff, opened several new China offices, and added numerous new products to assist clients needing to learn more about human resources in China.

Hala Helmy, President, Mundipharma, Beijing. Ms. Helmy arrived in Beijing in 2003 after 12 years working in the pharmaceutical industry. She served as General Manager of Mundipharma Beijing until 2007 when she left to become Managing Director of the International Handball Federation in Basel, Switzerland. Ms. Helmy is a Swiss national with both an MBA and an M.A. degree in Human Resources. She also holds diplomas in coaching and organizational development. Mundipharma is a joint venture between Mundipharma Pharmaceutical Company and Beijing Pharmaceutical Works. It employs 150 people in China.

Patrick Huang, Managing Director, Watson Wyatt Worldwide, Shanghai, China. Mr. Huang has been with Watson Wyatt for 15 years. He opened the Watson Wyatt Taiwan office and has led it to become one of the top service innovators and most profitable Watson Wyatt offices. In 2001, after living in Taiwan for more than 50 years, he returned to his birthplace, Shanghai, to run Watson Wyatt's Greater China operations. He has already grown the employee and revenue sizes of these operations and is trying to reproduce the success of the Taiwan operations. Before joining Watson Wyatt, Mr. Huang worked as Director of Human Resources for a British chemical company for 12 years.

Victor Lang, President, MMD Asia Pacific Ltd., Beijing. Mr. Lang was born and raised in mainland China. He has been the President of MMD Asia since 1997 when he started the China operations from scratch. MMD is a British firm that manufactures a variety of heavy machinery products used in various mining industries. Mr. Lang views himself as a leader who takes what he has learned from the West and applies it in ways that work in China. He prides himself on keeping his cell phone turned on 24 hours a day, seven days a week. He believes clients in China demand this. He sees this as distinguishing him from many Western leaders, who may have a better work–life balance but are not as available to their clients as most Chinese are. He sees the leadership role in China as very public. Leaders (like the former emperors) have very little privacy in their lives. If the boss works hard, the employees will follow, he believes. Mr. Lang has a bachelor's degree from the University of Central China and an MBA from the European International Business School. He has worked in the US, Europe, China, and other countries in Asia.

Jim Leininger, General Manager, Watson Wyatt Worldwide, Beijing. Mr. Leininger's experience in China stretches back over 15 years. He has worked as a trainer and a consultant in China since the early 1990s. He is fluent in Mandarin and is considered by many in China as a dependable "China hand." His consulting work is focused on developing human capital for firms operating in China. In addition to his consulting work, he has led several human resources research projects in China and has written articles and spoken at professional conferences on many occasions. His bachelor's degree is from Valparaiso University in Indiana. He holds a master's degree in East Asian Studies from Stanford University in California and has undertaken intensive language training at universities in Taiwan and Beijing.

(James) Li Jianbo, Vice President, Human Resources, Cisco Systems (China), Beijing. Mr. Li has been with Cisco since early 2005. His emphasis is on leadership development and talent management. Prior to Cisco, Mr. Li was a senior executive at AsiaInfo where he focused on delivering business intelligence solutions to companies in Greater China. He has also held human resources leadership positions with IBM and Lucent. In 2003, Mr. Li was President of the Human Resource Association in Beijing and has been on the board of this organization since 1996. In 2000, he was awarded the title of "Best Human Resources Manager in China" by *China Staff* magazine. His bachelor's degree is in Computer Science from Tsinghua University in Beijing. He has also earned an MBA from Rutgers University in the US.

Ren Binyan, Ph.D., Vice President, Alcoa (China) Investment Company, Ltd., Beijing. Dr. Ren began his career at Alcoa as

Chief Representative in Beijing in 2002. He currently works as a senior executive for Alcoa in New York. Just prior to leaving for New York in 2007, Dr. Ren was in charge of the Alcoa Technical Center in Beijing. In that capacity, he was the "front face" for Alcoa with the Chinese government. He was born and raised in Harbin, China. During the Cultural Revolution, he spent three years in the countryside. Dr. Ren is one of the best-known figures in the aluminum industry in China. He has spent his career in positions in the US, Australia, and China. He has a master's degree and a Ph.D. from Washington State University.

Charles Shao, Director of Leadership Consulting, Hewitt Associates, Beijing.   Mr. Shao was born and raised in Shanghai. He began his professional work in corporate HR after completing his bachelor's degree studies in Shanghai. After a few years of corporate work, he went to Holland to achieve an MBA at the Rotterdam School of Management at Erasmus University. This program was very international in focus and prepared him for the wide diversity of Chinese and multinational clients he serves in China. His own experience with this variety of clients has convinced him that the best leaders in China are those who can blend their Chinese wisdom with the best of Western management practices.

Shi Lan, Senior Consultant for Leadership, Towers Perrin, Beijing. Ms. Shi has worked as a senior consultant in Beijing for several years. She has been a member of several prominent international consulting firms, including Hewlett Packard Consulting and Hewitt Associates, as well as her current role with Towers Perrin. At Hewitt Associates, she was a key member of the Asia Leadership Consulting Group. Ms. Shi has consulted in numerous industries in the US, the UK, and China. She obtained her bachelor's degree in China and graduate degrees from the Massachusetts Institute of Technology and Syracuse University.

Kelly Wang, Founder and Director, GW Technologies Co., Ltd., Beijing.   Mr. Wang is a Chinese national who has spent his entire career working on the China mainland in both Chinese and multi-national firms. Before founding GW Technologies with two partners in 1984, he worked primarily in the banking industry. GW Technologies is a high-tech company serving the telecommunications industry in China. It is currently expanding its services to foreign firms. Mr. Wang attributes his "egalitarian" leadership style to what he learned from his first boss, a Hong Kong Chinese man who emphasized the importance of people over processes. He has tried to follow that example throughout his own leadership career. The Chinese word *zong* (总, chief), which is an honorific title attached to a leader's name, is not used in his firm. He believes the word detracts from the egalitarian culture he wants to espouse.

Angie Wei, Senior Leadership Consultant, Hewitt Associates, Beijing. Ms. Wei has over 15 years' experience in leadership and talent management strategy, leadership assessment and development, training, business management, and operations. She was born in Shanghai and, as a young girl, moved with her family to Beijing where she has lived ever since. Ms. Wei received her college and graduate degrees in China. She holds a Master of Science in Telecommunications and Electronic Systems from the Beijing University of Posts and Telecom, as well as an EMBA from CEIBS. She made the decision to change paths from telecoms executive to leadership consultant a few years ago. Ms. Wei believes that there are many Chinese leaders who have the potential to be better and higher-level leaders, but says they are held back by a combination of cultural barriers and interpersonal shortfalls that they must overcome in order to progress. Ms. Wei devotes her consulting work to helping this group improve their leadership ability and potential.

(Chris) Xu Fang, Vice President, TCL Institute of Leadership Development, TCL Corporation, Huizhou. In heading up TCL's Leadership Development Institute, Ms. Xu is the primary individual at TCL designing leadership talent development strategies, implementing executive training, and coordinating leadership development with outside universities and consulting firms. She has been with TCL since 2004. Prior to TCL, she was a human resources executive with both private firms and state-owned enterprises in South China. Ms. Xu has degrees in Economics and English literature from two separate Chinese universities. She also holds an MBA degree from the New York Institute of Technology in the US.

Yi Min, Director of Global Leadership and Organization Development, Lenovo Group, Raleigh, North Carolina. Ms. Yi has worked with Lenovo since 2003. Before taking her current position in the US, she was the Director of Learning and Culture Development for Lenovo in Beijing. In her present role, she is responsible for implementing a global talent development program throughout the Lenovo world. She also participates in designing global leadership and management development programs for Lenovo's executives worldwide. She is especially concerned with the development of Chinese leaders to become global leaders in the firm. Prior to Lenovo, Ms. Yi was employed in positions related to leadership development, as well as in general marketing. These positions were all with multinational firms. Her bachelor's degree in Economics was earned at the Beijing United University.

Janet Zhong, Vice President, Human Resources, Asia Pacific, Alcoa (China) Investment Company, Ltd., Beijing. Ms. Zhong has been with Alcoa since 2004. She was hired to lead the talent management and organization development function until she was promoted to her current role in 2007. Prior to joining Alcoa, she worked with PepsiCo in China. In her current role, she oversees all human resources functions for Alcoa in the Asia region. She is a past recipient of the "HR Manager of the Year" award from *China Staff* magazine. Ms. Zhong received her MBA degree from Henley Management College in the UK.

Appendix 2

KEY CHINESE CONCEPTS RELEVANT TO LEADERSHIP IN CHINA

Many Chinese terms and concepts were used in this book. This appendix provides a summary of those concepts.

Ba Ling Hou (八零后): *After 1980.* This term is used to refer to those people who were born after 1980, whose cultural and work values are closer to those of Westerners. If they were born in one of the big cities, they are also part of China's "one-child policy." As such, they are likely to have come from families that treat them in a special way. Also, their parents may have been part of the rising middle class in China. These parents would have had more expendable cash than preceding generations and would often have spent that money on their only child. Many human resources leaders in China describe these employees as "little emperors or empresses." They tend to be more difficult to manage and to retain than employees born earlier than the 1980s.

Di Diao (低调): *Low-key.* This is a colloquialism that some Chinese leaders use to distinguish themselves from "show-offs." Many

Chinese believe that a low-key style is preferable to that of the typically more flashy Westerner.

Guan Xi (关系): *Relationship.* This is often the first Chinese concept that Westerners learn in China. Literally, it refers to relationships. But the meaning goes much deeper. *Guan xi* relationships are long-term ones, often spanning generations. Also, these relationships are reciprocal. People use *guan xi* in China for business in making introductions to potential clients or vendors, in hiring staff, in winning contracts, in court cases, and in any other situation where knowing someone may bring favor to the firm (or to one of its individual members). Westerners complain that *guan xi* is often used for negative purposes, such as to get around regulations or bribe officials—other practices that are considered either bad form or even illegal in Western cultures.

Hai Gui (海龟): *Sea turtle.* This term is used to refer to those Chinese who left China to work or study abroad and then returned. It is not necessarily negative, although there is often a sense that these people are frowned upon slightly by those who stayed behind. In the first few years of this century, these employees were highly sought after and were usually paid a higher salary than their colleagues who had not lived abroad. These days, their primary value lies in the experience they may have gained by working in a foreign firm. Otherwise, they are typically rewarded in China at the same rate as those who graduated from good Chinese schools.

Jue Ce Hui (决策会): *A meeting called to make a strategic decision.* Usually, the decision has already been made, and the meeting is called to make it official. But it can also be called for the purpose of coming to a conclusion and finalizing a decision. Such a meeting can be an important event in a Chinese business if a decision is required but cannot be made through consensus discussions alone.

Jun Jun Chen Chen Fu Fu Zi Zi (君君臣臣 父父子子): *King is king, minister is minister, father is father, and son is son.* For business leaders, this Confucian proverb means that when everyone has his or her rightful place in society, there is social order. Disorder arises when the reorganized hierarchy is broken. This call to hierarchy is fundamental to Confucianism. Some would argue that this approach hinders empowerment of the individual, which is valued more highly in the West than in China.

Jun Zi (君子): *Gentleman*. This is a Confucian concept and is considered the most admired style. Such people are of noble character. They are kind and benevolent. Leaders who are *junzi* are humble, tolerant, patient, and patriotic, and have a sincere desire for corporate harmony. Others typically see such a person as one who greatly respects his or her own family and the families of his or her employees.

Li (礼): *Rite*. In the religious sense, rites are rules. However, the Confucian meaning goes a step further. A person who follows *li* is polite and proper, and understands everyone's correct place in society. These rituals help to slot people into their proper place in the social hierarchy.

Mian Zi (面子): *Face*. People from all cultures are concerned with their reputation and self-respect. In China, as in most Asian cultures, however, *face* takes on a deeper meaning. Chinese people have a cultural and social mandate to maintain face in all their transactions. Considerations are taken before most transactions to ensure that neither party loses face.

Pai Ban (拍板): *Rap the gavel*. This means that someone (usually the leader) will make a final decision. It is like the judge rapping the gavel in court. It is often used after long deliberation when a decision must be made but there does not seem to be a likely conclusion unless someone exercises *pai ban*.

Qi Qi Ji (七七级): *Class of '77*. This was the first college class after Mao Zedong's Cultural Revolution. During the Cultural Revolution, universities in China were essentially shut down. After Mao's death, they were re-opened and a select group of students was admitted. All of these graduates shared a recent history of toiling in the fields and tending to agrarian chores, rather than engaging in scholarly pursuits. After graduation, nearly all of these graduates were assigned to positions in Chinese state-owned enterprises.

Qiang Da Chu Tou Niao (枪打出头鸟): *The first bird out gets shot.* This is the opposite of the Western saying, "The early bird catches the worm." It suggests taking a cautious approach. For leaders, it implies waiting until others have made their points before you make yours.

Ren (仁): *Humaneness and love of one's fellow man.* Confucius instructed people to be kindhearted, charitable, compassionate, and merciful. Beyond one's personal behavior, a person with *ren* is concerned with human welfare and the elimination of suffering in others and will be driven by an ethical code to improve humanity.

Ren Qing (人情): *Human feelings or sensibilities.* In business, however, this term is used to describe a practice of offering and accepting favors. These can be quite small, but they are often recalled by the giver and the recipient and are expected to be reciprocated. *Ren qing* is an important part of the *guan xi* relationships described earlier.

Tao Guang Yang Hui (韬光养晦): *Hiding your capabilities.* This is usually done to protect yourself from others whom you do not wish to know more about you than is necessary. This concept was practiced in China for centuries in order not to stand out and therefore be a potential target for attack. It is not common among leaders in China today except in state-owned enterprises.

Wu (悟): *Very deep insight.* This is a Buddhist concept. The Chinese character has the heart on the left and then, on the right, the five senses sitting atop the mouth. The implication is that someone with *wu* will use his or her mouth to ask questions and then use all of his or her senses and heart to fully understand something. Many Chinese believe that Westerners cannot do this well because they are taught to think in a linear fashion.

Wu Wei Er Zhi (无为而治): *Governing by doing nothing.* The implication is that a great leader will provide employees with what is necessary to get the job done, but will not stifle them with specific instructions, rules, and regulations. This is derived from *wu wei* (五位)—*the less the king does, the more that is done.* For leadership, the lesson is that if the leader provides a strong base, everyone else will handle the details and the company will be run well. If the leader gets too involved, however, there is bound to be confusion and disorder.

Xian Jiao Peng You Hou Zuo Sheng Yi (先交朋友 后做生意): *First make friends and then do business.* Many Chinese believe that it is important to be friends before doing business. This is an old view that is gradually changing. But the concept remains in the culture. This is very different from the Western approach, which encourages getting down to business as soon as possible.

Yi (义): *Moralty and uprightness.* In the Confucian sense, a person with *yi* lives a righteous life and believes in justice. He or she does what is morally right at all times.

Zheng Ti Guan Nian (整体观念): *Holistic thinking.* Generally, Westerners think in a linear fashion. There is logic and an order to their problem-solving and decision-making. The Chinese think holistically. The reasoning process follows no particular order. There are many cultural reasons for this difference between the Chinese and Western approaches to thinking, but it is often a source of conflict.

Zhong Jian Ren (中间人): *Middleman.* Middlemen are often used in China for a variety of purposes. Chinese leaders commonly use middlemen to perform tasks that they prefer not to handle directly. It may be to negotiate additional points in a deal, or perhaps to provide negative information about an arrangement. Chinese leaders, unlike Western leaders, prefer to leave these awkward issues to middlemen to avoid the risk of losing face or causing the other party to lose face.

Zhong Yong (中庸): *In the middle.* The actual meaning for leaders is: to not go to extremes. Confucius urged that a safe middle ground be found for all positions. There are many Chinese proverbs that espouse taking a middle-of-the-road approach. This idea, which most Chinese support, is often the cause of disputes with Westerners, whose own cultural upbringing has taught them to believe in the importance of taking sides and forging ahead in a particular direction. The concept is also related to the Daoist ideas of balance and harmony.

Zong (总): *Chief, president, or general manager.* The word is used before other words to indicate "the head of." For example, *zong du* (总督) means governor general, *zong li* (总理) means prime minister, and *zong lingshi* (总领事) means consul general. It is also used as an honorific after someone's name; for example, *Wang zong* literally means "Boss Wang" or "Chief Wang." Unlike in Western firms, where the leader tries to be as egalitarian as possible (especially in low power-distance cultures), this honorific usage is common in most Chinese companies.

BIBLIOGRAPHY

Abrashoff, D. Michael. *It's Your Ship* (New York: Warner Books, 2002).

Badarracco, Joseph L., Jr. *Leading Quietly: An Unorthodox Guide to Doing the Right Thing* (Boston, MA: Harvard Business School Publishing, 2002).

Balfour, Frederik. "China Vanke Company," *Architectural Record*, April 2008.

Becker, Jasper. *The Chinese* (New York: The Free Press, 2000).

Bennett, Mick and Andrew Bell. *Leadership Talent in Asia* (Singapore: John Wiley & Sons (Asia), 2004).

Bernthal, Paul R., Jason Bondra, and Wei Wang. *Leadership in China* (Pittsburgh, PA: Development Decisions International, 2005).

Buswell, Robert E., Jr. (ed.). *Chinese Buddhist Apocrypha* (Honolulu: University of Hawaii Press, 1990).

Campbell, Joseph. *The Power of Myth* (New York: Anchor Books, 1991).

Chan, Wing-Tsit. *A Sourcebook in Chinese Philosophy* (Princeton, NJ: Princeton University Press, 1969).

"China: Help Wanted," *Newsweek*, October 31, 2005, pp. E22–23.

Cohen, Ed. *Leadership Without Borders* (Singapore: John Wiley & Sons (Asia), 2007).

Covey, Stephen R. *The 7 Habits of Highly Effective People* (New York: Fireside, 1989).

DeKrey, Steven J. and David M. Messick (eds.). *Leadership Experiences in Asia* (Singapore: John Wiley & Sons (Asia), 2007).

Deloitte Touche Tohmatsu and The Economist Intelligence Unit. "Aligned at the Top," Deloitte Development LLC, 2007.

Earley, P. Christopher and Soon Ang. *Cultural Intelligence* (Stanford, CA: Stanford University Press, 2003).

Ebrey, Patricia Buckley. *China* (London: Cambridge University Press, 1996).

"Enhancing Emotional Intelligence to Create a High-performing Organization," *Chief Executive China*, January 2006, pp. 36–42.

Fernandez, Juan Antonio and Laurie Underwood. *China CEO* (Singapore: John Wiley & Sons (Asia), 2006).

Forney, Matthew. "Li Dongsheng: TCL," *Time.com*, December 17, 2004.

Fukuyama, Francis. *Trust: The Social Virtues and the Creation of Prosperity* (New York: The Free Press, 1995).

Fung, Yulan. *A Short History of Chinese Philosophy* (New York: The Free Press, 1948).

Gandossy, Robert and Jeffrey Sonnenfeld. *Leadership and Governance from the Inside Out* (Hoboken, NJ: John Wiley & Sons, 2004).

Gandossy, Robert and Marc Effron. *Leading the Way* (Hoboken, NJ: John Wiley & Sons, 2004).

George, Bill, Peter Sims, Andrew N. McLean, and Diana Mayer. "Discovering Your Authentic Leadership," *Harvard Business Review*, February 2007.

Goldsmith, Marshall and Laurence Lyons. *Coaching for Leadership* (San Francisco: John Wiley & Sons, 2006).

Goleman, Daniel. *Emotional Intelligence* (New York: Bantam Books, 1995).

Goleman, Daniel. "Leadership That Gets Results," *Harvard Business Review*, March–April 2000, p. 78.

Goleman, Daniel, Richard Boyatzis, and Annie McKee. *Primal Leadership: Realizing the Power of Emotional Intelligence* (Boston, MA: Harvard Business School Publishing, 2002).

Goleman, Daniel. "What Makes a Great Leader?" *Best of HBR 1998—Harvard Business Review*, January 2004.

Graham, John L. and N. Mark Lam. "The Chinese Negotiation," *Harvard Business Review*, Vol. 81, No. 10, October 2003, pp. 82–91.

Heidrick & Struggles with The Economist Intelligence Unit. *Executive Leadership in China* (London: July 2006).

Hewitt Associates. *Best Employers Survey*, 2005.

Hewitt Associates. "Leadership Development in China: Learning from Top Asian Companies (Internet report), Lincolnshire, Ill.: December 2003.

Hoffmann, W. John and Michael J. Enright (eds.). *China into the Future* (Singapore: John Wiley & Sons (Asia), 2008).

Hofstede, Geert. *Cultures and Organizations: Software of the Mind* (London: McGraw-Hill, 1991).

Hofstede, Geert and Michael H. Bond. "Confucius and Economic Growth: New Trends in Culture's Consequences," *Organizational Dynamics*, Vol. 16, No. 4, 1988, pp. 4–21.

Holstein, William J. "Best Companies for Leaders," *Chief Executive*, November 2005.

House, Robert J., Paul J. Hanges, Mansour Javidan, Peter W. Dorfman, and Vipin Gupta. *Culture, Leadership and Organizations* (Thousand Oaks, CA: Sage Publications, 2004).

House, Robert J., Paul J. Hanges, S. Antonio Ruiz-Quintanilla, Peter W. Dorfman, Mansour Javidian, Marcus Dickson, and Vipin Gupta. "Cultural Influences on Leadership and Organizations: Project GLOBE," a Monograph. www.Thunderbird.edu (2002).

"India's Edge," *Newsweek*, October 31, 2005, p. E25.

Jin, Ming Hui. "Selflessness—The Culmination of Leadership," *China HRD Net*. July 15, 2004.

Joerres, Jeffrey. "Managing China's Workforce," *Asian Wall Street Journal*, February 12, 2007, p. 13.

Kahl, Jack. *Leading from the Heart: Choosing to be a Servant Leader* (Westlake, OH: Kahl & Associates, 2004).

Kellerman, Barbara. "Yin and Yang of Leadership in China," *Compass*, 2006, p. 5.

Klann, Gene. "Leadership Character: Five Essential Characteristics," *Center for Creative Leadership*, Greensboro, NC (Podcast: www.ccl.org/leadership/podcast).

Koch, Tomas and Oliver Ramsbottom. "A Growth Strategy for a Chinese State-owned Enterprise," *McKinsey Quarterly*, July 2008.

Kouzes, James M. and Barry Y. Posner. *The Leadership Challenge*, 3rd edition (San Francisco: Jossey-Bass, 2002).

Kouzes, James M. and Barry Y. Posner. *A Leader's Legacy* (San Francisco: Jossey-Bass, 2006).

Krzyzewski, Mike, Donald T. Phillips, and Grant Hill. *Leading from the Heart: Coach K's Successful Strategies for Basketball, Business, and Life* (Victoria, Australia: Warner Books, 2001).

Landsberg, Max. *The Tao of Coaching* (London: Profile Books, Ltd., 2003).

Lang, Charlie. *The Groupness Factor* (Hong Kong: Progress-U Limited, 2005).

Lin, Yi Zhong (interview). "An Equation for Going Global," *Business Watch*, March 5, 2007, pp. 53–54.

Lin, Yu Tang. *My Country and My People* (Beijing: Foreign Language Teaching and Research Press, 1998).

Ling, Xhijun. *The Lenovo Affair* (Singapore: John Wiley & Sons (Asia), 2006).

Littrell, Romie F. "Desirable Leadership Behaviors of Multi-Cultural Managers in China," *Journal of Management Development*, Vol. 21, No. 1, 2002, pp. 5–74.

Lu, Xin Zhi. "Back to Basics," *Manager*, No. 152, March 1, 2007, p. 24.

Lynton, Nandani. "Challenges for the Chinese Executive," *Thunderbird*, Fall 2006, pp. 39–41.

McGregor, Douglas. *The Human Side of Intervention* (New York: McGraw-Hill, 1960).

Mansour, Javidian and Nandani Lynton. "The Changing Face of the Chinese Executive," *Harvard Business Review*, December 2005.

Michael, David. "Managing Rapid Growth," *Leadership.bcg.com*, February 2010.

Mo, Shao Kun. *Great Leadership* (Beijing: Oriental Press, 2006).

Morgan, Howard, Phil Harkins, and Marshall Goldsmith (eds.). *The Art and Practice of Leadership Coaching* (Hoboken, NJ: John Wiley & Sons, 2005).

Morrell, Margot and Stephanie Capparell. *Shackelton's Way* (New York: Penguin Books, 2001).

"Orient Group's Governance Puzzle," *China Business Review*, February 2007, No. 210, pp. 47–49.

Perkins, Dennis N. T. *Leading at the Edge* (New York: AMACOM, 2000).

Pfau, Bruce N. and Ira T. Kay. *The Human Capital Edge* (New York: McGraw-Hill, 2002).

Pittinsky, Todd L. and Cheng Zhu. "Contemporary Public Leadership in China: A Research Review and Considerations," John F. Kennedy School of Government, Harvard University, 2005.

Sun, Zhen Yao. "Objective Management Makes a Difference: How to Cultivate Employee Leadership Skills," *IT Manager's World*, December 5, 2006, pp. 114–115.

Sun, Zi. *The Art of War* (Internet; English translation found on various public websites).

Tichy, Noel M. *The Leadership Engine* (New York: HarperBusiness, 1997).

Wang, Mary Margaret, Richard W. Brislin, Wei-zhong Wang, David Williams, and Julie Haiyan Chao. *Turning Bricks into Jade* (Yarmouth, ME: Intercultural Press, Inc., 2000).

Warrilow, Jayne. "Leading from the Heart," *Ezine articles.com*, April 30, 2010.

Watson Wyatt Worldwide. *Work China* (Beijing: 2003).

Wei, Zhe. "Power, Control and the Leadership Temperament," *Manager in Shanghai*, No. 192, October 2005, p. 16.

Weldon, Elizabeth. "Chinese Leadership Models," CBIZ.CN (Internet), October 28, 2004.

"William Amelio Believes that Cross-cultural Thinking Will Turn Lenovo into China's First Successful Global Brand," *The Internet*, February 15, 2007.

Wright, Arthur F. *Studies in Chinese Buddhism*, ed. R. Somers (New Haven, CT: Yale University Press, 1990).

Yang, Ke Ming. *Chinese Characteristic Execution—OEC Management* (Beijing: Economy Publishing House, 2005).

Yang, Yuan Qing (interview). "Lenovo's Two Responsibilities for Going Global," *Business Watch*, March 5, 2007, pp. 51–52.

Yu, Lei. "Reasons for Clearing up the Mess," *China Business Review*, No. 210, February 2007, pp. 64–65.

Yu, Shi Wei. *The Leadership Quotient* (Beijing: Peking University Press, 2005).

Zeng, Shi Qiang. *The China Style of Leadership* (Beijing: Peking University Press, 2005).

Zhang, Chun Jiang (interview). "Looking for the Balance of In and Out," *Business Watch*, March 5, 2007, pp. 49–50.

Zhen, Ye Chen. "The Styles of Leadership that Employees Least Prefer," *Manager*, No. 152, March 1, 2007, pp. 36–40.

Zhijun, Ling. *The Lenovo Affair* (Singapore: John Wiley & Sons, 2006).

Zhou, Hao and Li Rong Long. "A Review of Paternalistic Leadership Research," *Advances in Psychological Sciences*, October 5, 2004, pp. 227–238.

Zhu, Jiang. *The Executive Handbook for Mid-Level Management* (Beijing: Peking University Press, 2006).

INDEX